JUST
5
INGREDIENTS

VEGETARIAN

An Hachette UK Company
www.hachette.co.uk

First published in Great Britain in 2015 by Hamlyn,
a division of Octopus Publishing Group Ltd,
Endeavour House, 189 Shaftesbury Avenue,
London WC2H 8JY

www.octopusbooks.co.uk
www.octopusbooksusa.com

Distributed in the US by Hachette Book Group,
1290 Avenue of the Americas, 4th and 5th Floors,
New York, NY 10020

Distributed in Canada by Canadian Manda Group,
664 Annette St., Toronto, Ontario, Canada M6S 2C8

Some of the recipes in this book have previously appeared in other books
published by Hamlyn.

ISBN 978 0 600 62842 2

Printed and bound in China.

10 9 8 7 6 5 4 3 2 1

Commissioning Editor Eleanor Maxfield
Senior Editor Leanne Bryan
Design Manager Eoghan O'Brien
Designer Jeremy Tilston
Production Controller Sarah Kramer

Standard level kitchen spoon and cup measurements are used in all recipes.

**Eggs should be large unless otherwise stated. The U.S. Food and Drug
Administration advises that eggs should not be consumed raw. This book
contains dishes made with raw or lightly cooked eggs. It is prudent for
more vulnerable people, such as pregnant and nursing mothers, people with
weakened immune systems, the elderly, babies, and young children, to avoid
uncooked or lightly cooked dishes made with eggs. Once prepared, these dishes
should be kept refrigerated and used promptly.**

Milk should be whole unless otherwise stated.

**Ovens should be preheated to the specific temperature; if using a convection
oven, follow manufacturer's instructions for adjusting the time and the temperature.**

**All microwave information is based on a 650-watt oven. Follow manufacturer's
instructions for an oven with a different wattage.**

**This book includes dishes made with nuts and nut derivatives. It is advisable
for customers with known allergic reactions to nuts and nut derivatives and
those who may be potentially vulnerable to these allergies, such as pregnant
and nursing mothers, people with weakened immune systems, the elderly,
babies, and children, to avoid dishes made with nuts and nut oils. It is also
prudent to check the labels of prepared Ingredients for the possible inclusion
of nut derivatives.**

JUST
5
INGREDIENTS

VEGETARIAN

MAKE LIFE SIMPLE WITH MORE THAN 100 RECIPES USING 5 INGREDIENTS OR FEWER

hamlyn

CONTENTS

INTRODUCTION

The recipes in this book have been chosen not only for their simplicity and great flavors, but also because they use just five or fewer main ingredients.

Applying a five-ingredient approach to cooking will help you create a repertoire of quick, easily adaptable dishes that are not only inexpensive and tasty, but also require little shopping and preparation. You will learn to master some basic recipes in record time and learn to appreciate that cooking for yourself is a satisfying and empowering process.

This will make life easier in several ways. Because the recipes are straightforward, there is less fussy preparation. The shopping lists are short and simple—how long do you really want to spend in a supermarket searching for something to cook? The five-ingredient approach is also economical and could help if you are on a budget— you won't be left with half-used packages of ingredients from recipes that you will never use.

Unlike the other five-ingredient cookbooks, the recipes don't use a lot of hidden extras. This series requires only 10 additional pantry items—easy-to-remember basics that you may already have at home, but are also relatively inexpensive to buy.

Start by stocking up on your pantry 10 (see page 11). Make sure you always have at least some of these—that way, you will be just five ingredients away from a decent meal at any time.

Next, choose a recipe that suits the time you have to cook, your energy levels, and your mood. Check which pantry ingredients you will need from the list. The five key ingredients you have to buy to complete the dish are clearly numbered.

One of the best ways to eat inexpensively is to avoid costly processed foods. Instead, you should choose basic ingredients, such as vegetables, rice, pasta, fish, and chicken, and build your meals around these. You should also try to avoid waste and not spend money on food that has to be thrown away because you run out of time to prepare it. Buy food that lasts and plan around the expiration dates of foods. If you can, freeze the leftovers for another day.

Plan your meals for the week ahead so you only need to go shopping once. When you get into this habit, the ingredients for each meal will be there whenever you need them.

Buy in bulk to get the best prices. Make time to shop around and compare prices in the nearest supermarket, online, your local stores, and on farmers' market stalls. Stick to buying fruit and vegetables that are in season. Not only will they be better value than exotic produce flown in from abroad, but you will also reduce your food miles. Finally, don't even think about spending precious cash on a supermarket's special offer unless it is something you will actually use. Three cans of sardines in mustard sauce for the price of one is a bargain only if you do eat them.

Today, being a vegetarian, cooking for a vegetarian in your family, or choosing to have a couple of meat-free days a week is easy, with supermarkets and health food stores offering ingredients for making tasty and satisfying vegetarian dishes.

Ingredients

For a vegetarian diet, avoiding certain products can be tricky. For example, animal fat and ingredients, such as gelatin, may be used in manufactured foods. Rennet, which is extracted from the stomach lining of cows, is often used in making cheese. Also, some jars of curry sauces may contain shrimp. In many cases, there are vegetarian alternatives to these ingredients, so it's advisable to take time to read the food labels.

Cheese

Cheese is a good source of protein for vegetarians, but always check the label to be sure that it is suitable for vegetarians and doesn't contain animal rennet. Some hard cheeses are still made with animal rennet, although increasingly cheese is being made with "microbial enzymes," widely used in the industry because they are a consistent and inexpensive coagulant.

The term "microbial enzyme" means that it is a synthetically developed coagulant, while the term "vegetable rennet" indicates one derived from a vegetable source. Soft cheeses are manufactured without rennet. Some cottage cheeses and yogurt, however, may contain gelatin, which is derived from animal sources.

The following cheeses are suitable for vegetarians and useful to keep in the refrigerator: goat cheese, feta, mozzarella, vegetarian cheddar, vegetarian pasta cheese (this is a great vegetarian alternative to Parmesan cheese, for use in risottos or pasta dishes), taleggio, and ricotta.

Protein

This can come from legumes, such as peas, beans, and lentils, which are excellent and inexpensive sources of protein and also contain minerals, such as iron, zinc, and calcium. Soy products, including tofu and some textured protein, contain a form of "mycoprotein" and are available as a ground meat substitute, burgers, fillets, and sausages. Eggs, dairy products, nuts, and seeds are also good sources—they contain valuable zinc, calcium, and iron, as well as protein.

Iron

Iron is vital for the maintenance of healthy red blood cells and to prevent anemia. Vegetarian sources include eggs, leafy green vegetables, wheat bread, molasses, dried fruit (especially apricots),

legumes, breakfast cereals that have been fortified, peanut butter, and pumpkin, sesame, and sunflower seeds. Iron that comes from vegetable sources is not as easily absorbed as that from animal sources. If eaten with food rich in vitamin C, the body's absorption of iron is enhanced. Drink fruit juice with breakfast cereal or squeeze fresh lemon juice over green vegetables and salads.

WEEKLY PLANNER

INDULGE YOURSELF

MONDAY
Tomato & feta tart (see page 62)

TUESDAY
Beet & goat cheese casserole (see page 78)

WEDNESDAY
Red rice & squash risotto (see page 156)

THURSDAY
Shallot tart tatin (see page 142)

FRIDAY
Sweet & sour ginger tofu (see page 158)

SATURDAY
Red onion & goat cheese tart (see page 134)

PANTRY 10

The only extras you will need!

1   Sugars
2   Flours
3   Oils & vinegars
4   Baking powder
5   Salt
6   Black pepper
7   Stock or broth
8   Onion
9   Garlic
10 Lemon & lemon juice

SHOPPING LIST:

Fruit & vegetables

- 2 cups baby plum or roma tomatoes (about 8 oz)
- 12 beets (about 2 lb)
- 1 butternut squash or 1½ lb pumpkin
- 1 lb shallots

Herbs & spices

- 1 bunch of basil
- ½ teaspoon caraway seeds
- 1 tablespoon lemon thyme
- 1 bunch of thyme
- 10 oz fresh ginger root
- small bunch of fresh cilantro leaves

Dairy

- 4 oz feta cheese
- 4 oz Parmesan cheese
- 1 stick unsalted butter
- 14 oz soft round goat cheese
- ½ cup heavy cream
- 3 eggs

Jars, cans, packages

- 3 (1 lb) pages ready-to-bake puff pastry
- 3 tablespoons pesto
- 1¼ cups Camargue red rice or long-grain brown rice
- 1 lb firm tofu (bean curd)
- 2 tablespoons light soy sauce
- 3 tablespoons tamarind paste (or 2 tablespoons lime juice)
- 6 oz semisweet chocolate
- unsweetened cocoa powder, for dusting

SUNDAY
Rich chocolate mousse (see page 178)

WEEKLY PLANNER

ON A BUDGET

MONDAY
Red pepper soup (see page 34)

TUESDAY
Mushroom stroganoff (see page 82)

WEDNESDAY
Spinach & potato omelet (see page 118)

THURSDAY
Spiced chickpeas with kale (see page 116)

FRIDAY
No-cook-tomato spaghetti (see page 88)

SATURDAY
Caldo verde (see page 38)

PANTRY 10

The only extras you will need!

1 Sugars
2 Flours
3 Oils & vinegars
4 Baking powder
5 Salt
6 Black pepper
7 Stock or broth
8 Onion
9 Garlic
10 Lemon & lemon juice

SUNDAY
Roasted tomato & mozzarella salad (see page 56)

SHOPPING LIST:

Fruit & vegetables

- 3 red bell peppers
- 2 zucchini
- 1 lb cremini mushrooms
- 8 oz new potatoes
- 1 (6 oz) package baby spinach leaves
- 4 oz curly kale
- 6 very ripe tomatoes (about 1½ lb)
- ¼ small head dark green cabbage
- 6 floury potatoes, such as russets (about 1½ lb)
- 2 cups baby plum or roma tomatoes (about 8 oz)
- 1 small package argula

Herbs & spices

- 1 bunch of chives
- 1 small bunch of parsley
- 1 bunch of basil
- 2 teaspoons fennel seeds
- 1 small bunch of cilantro

Dairy

- ½ cup plain yogurt or heavy cream
- 1 tablespoon butter
- ½ cup crème fraîche or plain Greek yogurt
- 6 extra-large eggs
- 1 lb mini mozzarella cheese balls

Jars, cans, packages

- 1 small jar whole-grain mustard
- 1 small jar mild curry paste
- 1 (14½ oz) can diced tomatoes
- 1 (15 oz) can chickpeas
- 1 (1 lb) package dried spaghetti
- 1 (15 oz) can cannellini beans, drained
- 3 tablespoons pine nuts

5 FOR PASTA

Pasta is everybody's favorite comfort food, but it's very easy to fall into the trap of cooking the same old pasta dishes. Use these 5-ingredient recipes as inspiration and to increase your pasta repertoire.

Delicatessen pasta salad (see page 36)

Spaghetti & zucchini frittata (see page 64)

Rigatoni with chile & basil tomato sauce (see page 98)

Basil & arugula pesto with spaghetti (see page 110)

Beet pasta with herbs (see page 114)

5 FOR ONE DISH

One-dish cooking is the ultimate easy way to cook. Instead of just tossing everything into a Dutch oven or casserole dish and hoping for the best, try out these one-dish recipes to create some fantastic easy meals.

Roasted stuffed red peppers (see page 74)

Melanzane parmigiana (see page 90)

Home baked beans (see page 106)

Mushroom & spinach lasagne (see page 138)

Red rice & squash risotto (see page 156)

5 FOR STARTING THE DAY

Get your day off to the brightest start with these delicious 5-ingredients vegetarian breakfast or brunch recipes. Whether you prefer something savory or sweet, this selection will hit the spot.

Pesto scrambled eggs (see page 66)

Corn & roasted pepper frittata (see page 84)

Potato hash browns with eggs (see page 92)

Home baked beans (see page 106)

Grilled bananas with blueberries (see page 182)

5 FOR POTATOES

Are you bored of always eating potatoes as an accompaniment to your vegetarian meal? Try these different potato recipes to change it up a little and make potatoes the focus, instead of the side dish, of your recipe.

New potato, basil & pine nut salad (see page 30)

Pea, potato & arugula soup (see page 40)

Spicy apple & potato soup (see page 46)

Asparagus & new potato tortilla (see page 70)

Baked sweet potatoes (see page 126)

5 FOR COOLING DOWN

These 5 summer-inspired recipes will have you thinking of sunshine, blue skies, and warm weather in no time. Cook them on a cold winter's day to bring a bit of summer into your life anytime of the year.

Summer green pea soup (see page 26)

Beet & orange salad (see page 44)

Fava bean & lemon spaghetti (see page 128)

Melon, ginger & lime sorbet (see page 166)

Summer berry sorbet (see page 168)

5 FOR A PICNIC

Always on the search for a great portable snack? These 5 picnic or lunch-box recipes will be a great source of inspiration. Make a couple of portions so that you have enough to last you through the week.

Bean, lemon & rosemary hummus (see page 104)

Tabbouleh with fruit & nuts (see page 108)

Spinach & potato omelet (see page 118)

Cold Asian summer soba noodle salad
(see page 146)

Wild rice & goat cheese salad (see page 148)

SOUPS & SALADS

SERVES 6

Preparation time 10 minutes
Cooking time 1 hour 5 minutes

INGREDIENTS

1 4 carrots, chopped

2 2 parsnips, chopped

3 1 leek, finely chopped

4 2 teaspoons thyme leaves

5 thyme sprigs, to garnish

PANTRY

olive oil, for spraying; 5 cups vegetable stock or broth; salt and black pepper

Roast Root Vegetable Soup

■ Put the carrots and parsnips into a roasting pan, spray lightly with olive oil, and season with salt and black pepper. Roast in a preheated oven, at 400°F, for 1 hour or until the vegetables are soft.

■ Meanwhile, 20 minutes before the vegetables have finished roasting, put the leek in a large saucepan with the stock or broth and 1 teaspoon of the thyme. Cover the pan and simmer for 20 minutes.

■ Transfer the roasted root vegetables to a blender or food processor and blend, adding a little of the stock or broth, if necessary. Transfer to the stock pan and season to taste. Add the remaining thyme, stir, and simmer for 5 minutes to reheat.

■ Ladle into individual bowls and serve garnished with the thyme sprigs.

SERVES 6

Preparation time 25 minutes
Cooking time 20 minutes

INGREDIENTS

| 1 | 6 ripe tomatoes (about 1½ lb) |

| 2 | 1 large baking potato, diced |

| 3 | 1 tablespoon tomato paste |

| 4 | small bunch of basil |

PANTRY

2 tablespoons olive oil; 1 onion, coarsely chopped; 2 garlic cloves, finely chopped; 3 cups vegetable or chicken stock or broth; 1 tablespoon packed light brown sugar; 4 teaspoons balsamic vinegar; salt and black pepper

Tomato & Balsamic Vinegar Soup

■ Cut the tomatoes in half, place them, cut side down, in an aluminum foil-lined broiler pan and drizzle with some oil. Broil for 4–5 minutes, until the skins have split and blackened.

■ Meanwhile, sauté the onion, potato, and garlic in the remaining oil for 5 minutes, stirring occasionally until softened and turning golden around the edges.

■ Peel and coarsely chop the tomatoes and add to the onion and potato with the pan juices, then stir in the stock, tomato paste, brown sugar, and balsamic vinegar. Add half the basil, season, and bring to a boil. Cover and simmer for 15 minutes.

■ Puree half the soup, in batches, in a blender or food processor until smooth. Return to the saucepan with the rest of the soup and reheat. Season to taste, then ladle into bowls, garnish with the remaining basil leaves, and serve with Parmesan twists or cheese straws, if desired.

SERVES 4

Preparation time 10 minutes or longer if shelling
  fresh peas
Cooking time about 3 minutes

INGREDIENTS

1	1 tablespoon butter
2	3½ lb fresh peas in their pods, shelled, or 3½ cups frozen peas
3	2 tablespoons plain Greek yogurt or light cream
4	nutmeg, to taste
5	1 tablespoon chopped and 2 whole chives, to garnish

PANTRY

½ onion, chopped; 3 cups vegetable stock or broth

Summer Green Pea Soup

■ Melt the butter in a large saucepan and soften the onion, but do not let it brown. Add the peas to the pan with the stock or broth. Bring to a boil and simmer for 2–3 minutes for fresh peas and 3 minutes for frozen peas, until they are cooked. Be careful not to overcook fresh peas or they will lose their flavor.

■ Remove from the heat and puree in a blender or food processor. Grate in a little nutmeg. Reheat gently, if necessary, and serve with a swirl of yogurt or cream and the chopped and whole chives.

ADD FAVA BEANS & MINT

For minted pea and fava bean
soup, fry the onion in the butter as
in the main recipe, then add 625 g
(1¼ lb) fresh peas and 625 g (1¼ lb)
fresh fava beans, both podded
or 250 g (8 oz) frozen peas and
250 g (8 oz) frozen fava beans,
2 stems of fresh mint and the stock.
Simmer as in the main recipe then
puree, reheat and ladle into bowls.
Top with 4 tablespoons heavy
cream swirled into the soup and
a few tiny fresh mint leaves.

SERVES 4

Preparation time 10 minutes
Cooking time 20 minutes

INGREDIENTS

1	**2 celery sticks, thinly sliced**
2	**2 (15 oz) cans lima beans, rinsed and drained**
3	**¼ cup tomato paste**
4	**1 tablespoon chopped rosemary or thyme, plus extra sprigs to decorate**
5	**Parmesan cheese shavings, to serve**

PANTRY

3 tablespoons olive oil; 1 onion, finely chopped;
2 garlic cloves, thinly sliced; 4 cups vegetable
stock or broth; salt and black pepper

Lima Bean & Tomato Soup

■ Heat the oil in a saucepan. Add the
onion and sauté for 3 minutes, until
softened. Add the celery and garlic and
sauté for about 2 minutes.

■ Add the lima beans, tomato paste, stock
or broth, rosemary or thyme, and a little
salt and black pepper. Bring to a boil, then
reduce the heat, cover, and simmer gently
for 15 minutes. Serve sprinkled with the
Parmesan shavings and some rosemary
or thyme sprigs to garnish.

SERVES 4-6

Preparation time 5 minutes, plus cooling
Cooking time 15 minutes

INGREDIENTS

1	**2 lb new potatoes, scrubbed**
2	**⅓ cup pine nuts, toasted**
3	**½ bunch of basil leaves**

PANTRY

¼ cup extra virgin olive oil; 1½ tablespoons white
wine vinegar; salt and black pepper

New Potato, Basil & Pine Nut Salad

■ Put the potatoes into a large saucepan
of lightly salted water and bring to a boil.
Cook for 12–15 minutes, until tender. Drain
well and transfer to a large bowl.

■ Cut any large potatoes in half.

■ Whisk the oil, vinegar, and a little salt
and black pepper together in a small bowl.
Add half to the potatoes, stir well, and
let cool completely.

■ Add the pine nuts, the remaining
dressing, and basil, stir well, and serve.

SERVES 4

Preparation time 20 minutes
Cooking time 30 minutes

INGREDIENTS

1 1 fennel bulb, thinly sliced

2 1 potato, diced

3 ¼ cup chopped parsley

4 16 black Greek olives, pitted and chopped

PANTRY

⅓ cup extra-virgin olive oil, plus extra for drizzling; 1 onion, chopped; finely grated zest of 2 lemons, plus juice of 1 lemon; 4 cups vegetable stock or broth; 1 small garlic clove, finely chopped; salt and black pepper

Fennel Soup with Black Olive Gremolata

■ Heat the oil in a large saucepan, add the onion, and cook for 5–10 minutes or until beginning to soften. Add the fennel, potato, and zest of 1 lemon and cook for 5 minutes, until the fennel begins to soften. Pour in the stock and bring to a boil. Reduce the heat, cover the pan, and simmer for about 15 minutes or until the vegetables are tender.

■ Meanwhile, to make the gremolata, mix together the garlic, the remaining lemon zest, and the parsley, then stir the chopped olives into the herb mixture. Cover and chill.

■ Blend the soup in a blender or food processor and pass it through a strainer to remove any strings of fennel. The soup should not be too thick, so add more stock, if necessary. Return it to the rinsed pan. Taste and season well with salt, black pepper, and plenty of lemon juice. Pour into warm bowls and sprinkle each serving with gremolata, to be stirred in before eating, and a drizzle of olive oil. Serve with slices of toasted crusty bread, if desired.

AN ITALIAN CLASSIC

For green olive and thyme gremolata, mix together 1 finely chopped garlic clove, finely grated zest of 1 lemon, ¼ cup chopped parsley, and 2 teaspoons chopped lemon thyme, then stir in 16 pitted and chopped green olives. Serve on the soup, cooked as in the main recipe, and drizzle with lemon-infused olive oil.

SERVES 4
....
Preparation time 15 minutes
Cooking time 35 minutes

INGREDIENTS
....

| 1 | 3 red bell peppers, seeded and coarsely chopped |

....

| 2 | 2 zucchini, finely chopped |

....

| 3 | plain yogurt or heavy cream |

....

| 4 | chopped chives |

PANTRY
....

2 onions, finely chopped; 2 tablespoons olive oil; 1 garlic clove, crushed ; 4 cups vegetable stock or broth; salt and black pepper

Red Pepper Soup

■ Put the onions in a large saucepan with the oil and gently sauté for 5 minutes or until softened and golden brown. Add the garlic and cook gently for 1 minute.

■ Add the red bell peppers and half the zucchini and sauté for 5–8 minutes or until softened and brown.

■ Add the stock to the pan with salt and black pepper and bring to a boil. Reduce the heat, cover the pan, and simmer gently for 20 minutes.

■ When the vegetables are tender, blend the mixture, in batches, in a blender or food processor to a smooth soup and return to the pan.

■ Season to taste, reheat, and serve topped with the remaining chopped zucchini and garnished with yogurt or a swirl of cream and chopped chives. This vibrant and warming soup is ideal for any meal and tastes just as good warm or cold.

Preparation time 10–15 minutes
Cooking time 10 minutes

INGREDIENTS

1 4 small–medium ripe tomatoes, cut into wedges

2 2 (10 oz) packages fresh spinach and ricotta tortellini

3 1 (9 oz) jar mixed sliced roasted peppers in olive oil

4 1 (9 oz) jar mushrooms in olive oil, drained

5 4 cups mixed baby greens and herb salad

PANTRY

black pepper

Delicatessen Pasta Salad

■ Put the tomato wedges in a single layer in an aluminum foil-lined broiler pan and broil under a preheated broiler for 2-3 minutes on each side.

■ Bring a large saucepan of lightly salted water to a boil. Add the tortellini and cook according to the package directions. Drain well and transfer to a large bowl.

■ Add the jar of mixed peppers, including the oil, along with the drained mushrooms and broiled tomatoes.

■ Add the baby greens and herb salad. Season with black pepper, stir gently to combine, and serve warm.

SERVES 4

Preparation time 15 minutes
Cooking time 35 minutes

INGREDIENTS

1 4 oz dark green cabbage,
such as cavolo nero (Tuscan kale)

2 6-7 russet potatoes (about 1½ lb),
cut into small chunks

3 1 (15 oz) can cannellini beans, drained

4 ½ oz fresh cilantro, coarsely chopped

PANTRY

¼ cup olive oil; 1 large onion, chopped;
2 garlic cloves, chopped; 4 cups vegetable stock
or broth; salt and black pepper

Caldo Verde

■ Trim off any tough stem ends from
the cabbage and roll the leaves up tightly.
Using a large knife, shred the cabbage as
finely as possible.

■ Heat the oil in a large saucepan and
gently sauté the onion for 5 minutes.
Add the potatoes and cook, stirring
occasionally, for 10 minutes. Stir in the
garlic and cook for another 1 minute.

■ Add the stock and bring to a boil.
Reduce the heat and simmer gently,
covered, for about 10 minutes, until the
potatoes are tender. Use a potato masher
to lightly mash the potatoes into the
soup so that they are broken up but not
completely pureed.

■ Stir in the beans, cabbage, and cilantro
and cook gently for another 10 minutes.
Season to taste with salt and black pepper.

AN IRISH FAVORITE

For "colcannon," boil 4 unpeeled russet potatoes until tender. Drain and add ⅔ cup milk. Meanwhile, boil 5 cups finely shredded green cabbage for 10 minutes or until the cabbage is tender. Drain and add 6 finely chopped scallions. When cool enough to handle, peel and mash the potatoes in a medium bowl, then beat in the cabbage and scallions. Season and beat in 4 tablespoons butter.

SERVES 4–6

Preparation time 15 minutes
Cooking time 35 minutes

INGREDIENTS

1   2 teaspoons chopped thyme

2   2–3 potatoes (about 8 oz), chopped

3   3½ cups frozen or fresh shelled peas

4   4 cups coarsely chopped arugula leaves

PANTRY

3 tablespoons extra virgin olive oil, plus extra
to serve; 1 onion, finely chopped; 2 garlic cloves,
finely chopped; 4 cups vegetable stock or broth;
juice of 1 lemon; salt and black pepper

Pea, Potato & Arugula Soup

■ Heat the oil in a saucepan, add the
onion, garlic, and thyme, and cook over
low heat, stirring frequently, for 5 minutes,
until the onion is softened. Add the
potatoes and cook, stirring frequently,
for 5 minutes.

■ Stir in the peas, stock or broth, and salt
and black pepper. Bring to a boil, then
reduce the heat, cover, and simmer gently
for 20 minutes.

■ Transfer the soup to a blender or food
processor, add the arugula and lemon
juice, and process until smooth. Return
to the pan, adjust the seasoning, and heat
through. Serve immediately, drizzled with
a little extra oil.

TRY IT WITH ASPARAGUS

For summer pea and asparagus soup, omit the potatoes and add 8 oz asparagus spears. Trim off the tips and cook them in the stock for 3–5 minutes, until tender. Drain and set aside, reserving the stock. Slice the remaining asparagus and add to the soup with the peas. Serve garnished with the tips.

SERVES 4

Preparation time 15 minutes
Cooking time 1¼ hours

INGREDIENTS

1 1 butternut squash

2 a few rosemary sprigs, plus extra to garnish

3 1 cup dried red lentils, washed

PANTRY

2 tablespoons olive oil; 1 onion, finely chopped; 4 cups vegetable stock or broth; salt and black pepper

Butternut Squash & Rosemary Soup

■ Cut the squash in half and use a spoon to scoop out the seeds and fibrous flesh. Peel and cut the squash into small chunks and place in a roasting pan. Sprinkle with the oil and rosemary, and season well with salt and black pepper. Roast in a preheated oven, at 400°F, for 45 minutes.

■ Meanwhile, place the lentils in a saucepan, cover with water, bring to a boil, and boil rapidly for 10 minutes. Strain, then return the lentils to a clean saucepan with the onion and stock and simmer for 5 minutes. Season to taste.

■ Remove the squash from the oven, mash the flesh with a fork, and add to the soup. Simmer for 25 minutes and then ladle into bowls. Garnish with more rosemary before serving.

SERVES 2-4

Preparation time 15 minutes
Cooking time 30 minutes

INGREDIENTS

1 7 small beets

2 2 oranges

3 1 teaspoon whole-grain mustard

4 ½ bunch of watercress or 2 cups arugula

5 3 oz soft goat cheese

PANTRY

1 tablespoon red wine vinegar; 1½ tablespoons white wine vinegar; 3 tablespoons olive oil; salt and black pepper

Beet & Orange Salad

■ Scrub and trim the beets and put them in an aluminum foil-lined roasting pan with the red wine vinegar and bake in a preheated oven, at 375°F, for 30 minutes or until cooked. Check by piercing one with a knife. Let the beets cool slightly and then, wearing food-handling gloves, rub off the skin and slice the globes into halves or quarters, if large.

■ Meanwhile, peel and segment the oranges. Make the dressing by whisking together the white wine vinegar, oil, and mustard. Season with salt and black pepper.

■ Put the watercress or arugula into a bowl with the beets and add the dressing. Mix gently to combine. Arrange the oranges on a plate, top with the beets and greens, and crumble the cheese on top. Season with black pepper and serve.

SERVES 4

Preparation time 15 minutes
Cooking time 30 minutes

INGREDIENTS

1 | 5 tablespoons butter

2 | 2 sweet, crisp apples, peeled, cored, and sliced, plus ½–1 sweet, crisp apple, peeled, cored, and diced, to garnish

3 | pinch of cayenne pepper (or to taste), plus extra for sprinking

4 | 3 Yukon gold or russet potatoes, sliced

5 | 1¼ cups hot milk

PANTRY

1 small onion, chopped; 2½ cups vegetable stock or broth; salt

Spicy Apple & Potato Soup

■ Melt 4 tablespoons of the butter in a large, heavy saucepan over medium heat. Add the onion and cook for 5 minutes or until softened. Add the 2 sliced apples and cayenne and cook, stirring, for another 2 minutes.

■ Pour in the stock or broth, then add the potatoes. Bring to a boil, reduce the heat, and simmer gently for 15–18 minutes, until the apples and potatoes are tender.

■ Blend the soup, in batches, in a blender or food processor until smooth, then transfer to a clean saucepan. Reheat gently and stir in the hot milk. Taste and adjust the seasoning, if necessary.

■ Meanwhile, make the apple garnish. Melt the remaining butter in a small skillet, add the diced apple, and cook over high heat until crisp.

■ Serve the soup in warm bowls, garnishing each portion with some diced apple and a sprinkling of cayenne.

SERVES 4

Preparation time 20 minutes
Cooking time 25 minutes

INGREDIENTS

1 ½ butternut squash or 1 lb pumpkin

2 2 thyme sprigs, coarsely chopped

3 1 (7 oz) package mixed baby salad greens

4 2 oz feta cheese

5 2 tablespoons toasted pine nuts, to garnish

PANTRY

2 tablespoons balsamic vinegar; ¼ cup olive oil, plus extra for drizzling; salt and black pepper

Squash, Feta & Pine Nut Salad

■ Skin and seed the butternut squash or pumpkin and cut the flesh into ¾ inch squares—you should have about 4 cups. Put the squash or pumpkin into a roasting pan. Drizzle with olive oil, sprinkle with the thyme, and season with salt and black pepper. Roast in a preheated oven, at 375°F, for 25 minutes or until cooked though. Remove the squash or pumpkin from the oven and let cool slightly.

■ Meanwhile, make the dressing. Whisk together the vinegar and ¼ cup of oil and set aside.

■ Put the mixed greens in a large salad bowl, add the cooked squash or pumpkin, and crumble in the feta. Drizzle with the dressing and toss carefully to combine. Transfer the mixture to serving plates, garnish with toasted pine nuts, and serve immediately.

SERVES 6

Preparation time 15 minutes
Cooking time 20 minutes

INGREDIENTS

1	3-4 leeks (about 12 oz), slit and well washed, then thinly sliced
2	2½ cups fresh shelled or frozen peas
3	small bunch of mint, plus a few leaves to garnish (optional)
4	⅔ cup mascarpone cheese

PANTRY

2 tablespoons olive oil; 4 cups vegetable stock or broth; grated zest of 1 small lemon, plus lemon zest curls to garnish (optional); salt and black pepper

Cream of Leek & Pea Soup

■ Heat the oil in a saucepan, add the leeks, toss in the oil, then cover and sauté gently for 10 minutes, stirring occasionally, until softened but not browned. Mix in the peas and cook briefly.

■ Pour the stock or broth into the pan, add a little salt and black pepper, then bring to a boil. Cover and simmer gently for 10 minutes.

■ Ladle half the soup into a blender or food processor, add all the mint, and blend until smooth. Pour the puree back into the saucepan. Mix the mascarpone with half of the lemon zest, reserving the rest to be used as a garnish.

■ Spoon half the mascarpone mixture into the soup, then reheat, stirring until the mascarpone has melted. Taste and adjust the seasoning, if needed. Ladle the soup into bowls and top with spoonfuls of the remaining mascarpone and a sprinkling of the remaining lemon zest. Garnish with mint leaves and lemon zest curls, if desired.

ADD WATERCRESS

For cream of leek, pea, and watercress soup, use just 1¼ cup peas and add a coarsely chopped bunch of watercress. Simmer in 2½ cups of stock or broth, then instead of adding the mascarpone, stir in ⅔ cup milk and ⅔ cup heavy cream, drizzling a little extra cream over at the end and topping with some crispy cooked and chopped bacon to garnish.

SERVES 4

Preparation time 15 minutes, plus resting
Cooking time 12 minutes

INGREDIENTS

1   8 oz malloreddus or orzo pasta

2   2 cups frozen peas, thawed

3   6 scallions, coarsely chopped

4   8 marinated artichoke hearts, thinly sliced

5   ¼ cup chopped mint

PANTRY

⅓ cup olive oil; 2 garlic cloves, crushed; zest
and juice of ½ lemon, plus grated lemon zest
to garnish; salt and black pepper

Warm Pasta Salad

■ Cook the pasta in a saucepan of lightly
salted boiling water for about 6 minutes
or according to the package directions.
Add the thawed peas and cook for another
2–3 minutes, until the peas and pasta are
cooked. Drain well.

■ Meanwhile, heat 2 tablespoons of oil in
a skillet and stir-fry the scallions and garlic
for 1–2 minutes, until softened.

■ Stir the scallions and garlic into the
pasta with the artichokes, mint, and
remaining oil. Toss well, season with
salt and black pepper, then let rest for
10 minutes. Stir in the lemon juice and serve
the salad warm, garnished with lemon zest.

SERVES 6

Preparation time 20 minutes
Cooking time 1–1¼ hours

INGREDIENTS

1   10 large carrots (about 1½ lb), diced

2   ¼ cup long-grain rice

3   1¼ cups milk

4   ¼ cup fresh mint, plus leaves to garnish (optional)

PANTRY

⅓ cup olive oil; 1 onion, coarsely chopped; 4 cups vegetable stock or broth; ¼ teaspoon sugar; salt and black pepper

Smooth Carrot Soup with Mint Oil

■ Heat 2 tablespoons of the oil in a saucepan, add the onion, and sauté for 5 minutes, until just beginning to soften and turn golden brown around the edges. Stir in the carrots and cook for 5 minutes. Mix in the rice, stock, and a little salt and black pepper. Bring to a boil, then cover and simmer for 45 minutes, stirring occasionally, until the carrots are cooked and tender.

■ Meanwhile, make the mint oil. Strip the leaves from the mint stems and add the leaves to a blender or food processor with the sugar and a little black pepper. Finely chop, then gradually blend in the remaining oil a little at a time with the motor running. Spoon into a small bowl and stir before using.

■ Rinse the blender or food processor, then puree the soup, in batches, until smooth. Return the soup to the saucepan and stir in the milk. Reheat, then taste and adjust the seasoning, if needed. Ladle into bowls, then drizzle with the mint oil and add some extra mint leaves, if using. Serve with muffins (see opposite), if desired.

MAKE SAVORY MUFFINS

For zucchini muffins, put 2½ cups all-purpose flour into a bowl and add 1 tablespoon baking powder, 1 cup freshly grated Parmesan cheese, 2 cups coarsely grated zucchini, ⅔ cup low-fat plain yogurt, 3 tablespoons olive oil, 3 eggs, and 3 tablespoons milk. Fork together until just mixed, and divide into a 12-cup muffin pan lined with paper liners. Bake in a preheated oven, at 400°F, for 18–20 minutes, until well risen and golden brown. Serve warm.

SERVES 4

Preparation time 10 minutes, plus cooling
Cooking time 20 minutes

INGREDIENTS

1 2 cups halved baby plum, roma, or cherry tomatoes

2 1 cup arugula leaves

3 12 basil leaves

4 5 oz mini mozzarella balls, drained

5 3 tablespoons pine nuts, toasted

PANTRY

1 tablespoon olive oil; ¼ cup extra virgin olive oil;
1 teaspoon red wine vinegar; salt and black pepper

Roasted Tomato & Mozzarella Salad

■ Place the tomatoes, cut side up, in a small roasting pan. Drizzle with 1 tablespoon of olive oil and season with a little sea salt and black pepper. Roast in a preheated oven, at 400°F, for 20 minutes, until wilted and softened. Remove from the oven and let cool.

■ Make the dressing. Put the arugula and basil leaves, 2 tablespoons of the extra virgin olive oil, and the vinegar into a small bowl. Blend with an immersion blender to a puree, or transfer to a mini food processor to blend. Stir in the remaining oil and season to taste with salt and black pepper.

■ Arrange the roasted tomatoes on a large plate, then tear the mozzarella balls in half and arrange among the tomatoes. Drizzle with the dressing and top with the pine nuts. Serve immediately.

CREATE A DRESSING

For basil dressing to serve as an alternative dressing for the salad, use 1 cup fresh basil leaves in place of the arugula and basil and follow the main recipe. Serve the salad with a handful of arugula leaves.

SERVES 6

Preparation time 15 minutes, plus soaking
Cooking time 30 minutes

INGREDIENTS

1 ½ bunch of flat-leaf parsley

2 1 (15 oz) can chickpeas, drained
and rinsed

PANTRY

1 small onion; 3 garlic cloves; 2 tablespoons olive
oil; 5 cups vegetable stock or broth; grated zest
and juice of ½ lemon; salt and black pepper

Chickpea & Parsley Soup

■ Put the onion, garlic, and parsley into
a food processor or blender and process
until finely chopped.

■ Heat the oil in a saucepan and cook the
onion mixture over low heat until slightly
softened. Add the chickpeas and cook
gently for 1–2 minutes.

■ Add the stock, season well with salt
and black pepper, and bring to a boil.
Cover and cook for 20 minutes or until
the chickpeas are tender. Let the soup
cool for a while, then partly puree it in a
food processor or blender or mash it with
a fork so that it retains plenty of texture.

■ Pour the soup into a clean saucepan,
add the lemon juice, and adjust the
seasoning, if necessary. Heat through
gently. Serve the soup topped with
grated lemon zest and black pepper.

TRY IT WITH BEANS

For great Northern, cannellini, and parsley soup, replace the chickpeas with 1 cup each canned or cooked great Northern and cannellini beans, and use the zest and juice of 1 lemon. Otherwise, cook as in the main recipe.

MIDWEEK MEALS

Preparation time 15 minutes
Cooking time 20 minutes

INGREDIENTS

1 1 sheet ready-to-bake puff pastry, thawed if frozen

2 3 tablespoons pesto

3 2 cups halved baby plum or roma tomatoes

4 ⅔ cup crumbled feta cheese

5 handful of basil leaves

PANTRY

all-purpose flour, for dusting; salt and black pepper

Tomato & Feta Tart

■ Roll the pastry out on a lightly floured work surface to form a 10 × 14 inch rectangle. Using a sharp knife, score a 1 inch border around the edges. Transfer to a baking sheet and spread the pesto over the pastry.

■ Arrange the tomatoes and feta over the top. Season with salt and black pepper. Bake in a preheated oven, at 425°F, for 20 minutes, until the pastry is puffed and golden. Remove from the oven and sprinkle with the basil leaves.

Preparation time 10 minutes
Cooking time 25 minutes

INGREDIENTS

1 2 zucchini, thinly sliced

2 4 eggs

3 4 oz spaghetti, cooked

4 ¼ cup freshly grated Parmesan cheese

5 10 basil leaves

PANTRY

2 tablespoons olive oil; 1 onion, thinly sliced;
1 garlic clove, crushed; salt and black pepper

Spaghetti & Zucchini Frittata

■ Heat the oil in a heavy, ovenproof, nonstick 9 inch skillet over low heat. Add the onion and cook, stirring occasionally, for 6–8 minutes, until softened. Stir in the zucchini and garlic and cook, stirring, for 2 minutes.

■ Beat the eggs in a large bowl and season with salt and black pepper. Stir in the cooked zucchini and garlic, spaghetti, and half the Parmesan and basil. Pour the mixture into the skillet and quickly arrange the ingredients so they are evenly dispersed. Cook over low heat for 8–10 minutes, or until all but the top of the frittata is set.

■ Transfer to a preheated hot broiler and place about 4 inches from the heat source. Cook until set but not browned.

■ Give the pan a shake to loosen the frittata, then transfer to a plate. Sprinkle the top with the remaining Parmesan and basil and let cool for 5 minutes before serving.

INGREDIENTS

1	12 eggs
2	½ light cream
3	2 tablespoons butter
4	4 slices of whole-grain bread, toasted
5	¼ cup pesto

PANTRY

salt and black pepper

Pesto Scrambled Eggs

■ Beat together the eggs, cream, and a little salt and black pepper in a bowl. Melt the butter in a large, nonstick skillet, add the egg mixture, and stir over low heat with a wooden spoon until cooked to your preference.

■ Put a slice of toast on each serving plate. Spoon one-quarter of the scrambled eggs onto each slice of toast, make a small indent in the center, and add a tablespoonful of pesto. Serve immediately.

MAKE IT CHEESY

For cheesy scrambled eggs, stir 4 oz diced soft goat cheese and 2 tablespoons chopped parsley into the eggs just before serving, and omit the pesto.

SERVES 4

Preparation time 10 minutes
Cooking time about 25 minutes

INGREDIENTS

1 2 eggplants, sliced in half lengthwise

2 1 cup canned diced tomatoes

3 1 tablespoon tomato paste

4 10 oz mozzarella cheese,
cut into 8 thin slices

5 basil leaves, to garnish

PANTRY

3 tablespoons olive oil; 1 onion, chopped; 1 garlic
clove, crushed; salt and black pepper

Baked Eggplants & Mozzarella

■ Brush the eggplants with 2 tablespoons
of the oil and arrange, cut side up, on a
baking sheet. Roast in a preheated oven,
at 400°F, for 20 minutes.

■ Meanwhile, heat the remaining oil in
a skillet, add the onion and garlic, and
cook until the onion is soft and starting
to brown. Add the tomatoes and tomato
paste and simmer for 5 minutes or until
the sauce has thickened.

■ Remove the eggplants from the oven
and cover each half with some sauce and
2 of the mozzarella slices. Season to taste
with salt and black pepper and return
to the oven for 4–5 minutes to melt the
cheese. Serve immediately sprinkled with
basil leaves.

SERVES 4

Preparation time 15 minutes
Cooking time 40 minutes

INGREDIENTS

1   12 oz asparagus spears

2   1 lb new potatoes

3   6 eggs

4   ¼ cup basil leaves, torn into pieces

PANTRY

½ cup olive oil; 1 onion, chopped; salt and black pepper

Asparagus & New Potato Tortilla

■ Snap the woody ends off the asparagus and cut the spears into 2 inch lengths. Slice the potatoes thinly.

■ Heat ¼ cup of the oil in a heavy skillet about 10 inches across. Add the asparagus and sauté gently for 5 minutes, until slightly softened. Lift out with a slotted spoon and transfer to a plate. Add the remaining oil to the pan with the potatoes and onion. Cook gently, turning often in the oil, for about 15 minutes, until the potatoes are tender.

■ Beat the eggs with a little salt and black pepper in a bowl and stir in the basil leaves. Add the asparagus to the pan and combine the vegetables so that they are evenly distributed. Pour the egg mixture over the vegetables and reduce the heat to its lowest setting. Cover with a lid or aluminum foil and cook for about 10 minutes, until almost set but still a little wobbly in the center.

■ Loosen the edge of the tortilla, cover the pan with a plate, and invert the tortilla onto it. Slide back into the pan and return to the heat for 2–3 minutes, until the bottom is firm. Slide onto a clean plate and serve warm or cold, cut into wedges, with Hollandaise sauce (see opposite), if desired.

A CLASSIC SAUCE

For hollandaise sauce, put
1 tablespoon white wine vinegar
in a food processor with 2 egg
yolks. Blend lightly to combine.
Cut 1¼ sticks butter into pieces and
melt gently in a small saucepan.
Pour into a small bowl. With the
machine running, slowly pour in
the melted butter until thick and
smooth. Season to taste with salt
and black pepper and add a dash
of hot water if the sauce is thick.
Spoon over the tortilla, if desired.

SERVES 2

Preparation time 15 minutes
Cooking time 10–12 minutes

INGREDIENTS

1   8 oz dried penne or other pasta shapes

2   1⅓ cups shelled fava beans, fresh or frozen

3   ⅓ cup drained and coarsely chopped sun-dried tomatoes in oil

4   handful of mixed herbs, such as parsley, tarragon, chervil, and chives, coarsely chopped

5   ⅓ cup crumbled or coarsely chopped feta cheese

PANTRY

2 tablespoons extra virgin olive oil; 1 tablespoon sherry vinegar; ½ garlic clove, crushed; salt and black pepper

Herbed Bean & Feta Salad

■ Cook the pasta in a large saucepan of salted boiling water according to the package directions until al dente. Drain, refresh in cold water, and drain thoroughly.

■ Meanwhile, cook the fava beans in a separate saucepan of lightly salted boiling water for 4–5 minutes, until just tender. Drain and plunge into ice-cold water to cool. Peel off the skins.

■ Make the dressing by whisking together the extra virgin olive oil, sherry vinegar, and garlic in a small bowl, then season with salt and black pepper.

■ Put the beans in a serving dish and stir in the pasta, tomatoes, and herbs. Toss with the dressing and sprinkle the feta cheese over the top. Serve immediately.

Preparation time 10 minutes
Cooking time 55–60 minutes

INGREDIENTS

1	**4 large red bell peppers**
2	**1 tablespoon chopped thyme, plus extra to garnish**
3	**4 plum or roma tomatoes, halved**

PANTRY

2 garlic cloves, crushed; ¼ cup extra virgin olive oil; 2 tablespoons balsamic vinegar; salt and black pepper

Roasted Stuffed Red Peppers

■ Cut the red bell peppers in half lengthwise, then scoop out and discard the cores and seeds. Put the bell pepper halves, cut sides up, in a roasting pan lined with aluminum foil or a ceramic dish. Divide the garlic and thyme between them and season with salt and black pepper.

■ Put a tomato half in each bell pepper half and drizzle with the oil and vinegar. Roast in a preheated oven, at 425°F, for 55–60 minutes, until the bell peppers are soft and charred.

Preparation time 10 minutes
Cooking time 20 minutes

INGREDIENTS

1	3 sweet potatoes (about 1 lb), sliced
2	5 scallions, sliced
3	2 tablespoons chopped fresh cilantro
4	4 extra-large eggs, beaten
5	4 oz goat cheese log with rind, cut into 4 slices

PANTRY

1 teaspoon olive oil; black pepper

Sweet Potato & Goat Cheese Frittata

■ Put the sweet potato slices into a saucepan of boiling water and cook for 7-8 minutes or until just tender, then drain.

■ Heat the oil in a medium, nonstick skillet, add the scallions and sweet potato slices, and sauté for 2 minutes.

■ Stir the cilantro into the beaten eggs, season with plenty of black pepper and pour into the pan. Arrange the slices of goat cheese on top and continue to cook for 3-4 minutes, until almost set.

■ Put the pan under a preheated hot broiler and cook for 2–3 minutes, until golden and bubbling. Serve immediately.

CHANGE THE FILLING

For butternut squash and feta frittata, replace the sweet potatoes with 500 g (1 lb) cubed butternut squash. Sprinkle 100g (3½ oz) of crumbled feta cheese on top of the frittata in place of the goat cheese.

Preparation time 25 minutes
Cooking time 1½ hours

INGREDIENTS

1 2 lb beets

2 ½ teaspoon caraway seeds

3 1 tablespoon chopped lemon thyme, plus extra to garnish

4 3 tablespoons butter, cut into small pieces

5 7 oz soft goat cheese, thinly sliced

PANTRY

7 small onions (about 1 lb), quartered; ¼ cup olive oil; ⅔ cup all-purpose flour; salt and black pepper

Beet & Goat Cheese Casserole

■ Scrub the beets and cut into thin wedges. Put them into a shallow ovenproof dish with the onions and drizzle with the oil. Sprinkle with the caraway seeds and season with a little salt and plenty of black pepper. Cook in a preheated oven, at 400°F, for about 1 hour, until the vegetables are roasted and tender, stirring once or twice during cooking.

■ Meanwhile, put the flour and lemon thyme into a bowl, add the butter, and rub in with the fingertips until the mixture resembles fine bread crumbs.

■ Sprinkle the goat cheese over the vegetables and sprinkle with the crumb mixture. Return to the oven for 25–30 minutes, until the topping is pale golden. Sprinkle the crumb topping with thyme and serve immediately.

Preparation time 10 minutes
Cooking time 10–15 minutes

INGREDIENTS

1 4 zucchini, cut into matchsticks

2 2 celery sticks, cut into matchsticks

3 1 cup cream cheese with garlic

4 1 cup walnut pieces

PANTRY

3 tablespoons olive oil; 1 onion, chopped; salt and
black pepper

Creamy Zucchini with Walnuts

■ Heat the oil in a large skillet, add the onion, and cook for 5 minutes, until soft. Add the zucchini and celery matchsticks and cook for 4–5 minutes, until soft and starting to brown.

■ Add the cheese and cook for 2–3 minutes, until melted. Stir in the walnuts, season to taste with salt and black pepper, and serve immediately.

SERVES 4

Preparation time 10 minutes
Cooking time 10 minutes

INGREDIENTS

1	1 tablespoon butter
2	1 lb cremini mushrooms, sliced
3	2 tablespoons whole-grain mustard
4	1 cup crème fraîche or sour cream
5	3 tablespoons chopped parsley

PANTRY

2 tablespoons olive oil; 1 onion, thinly sliced;
4 garlic cloves, finely chopped; salt and
black pepper

Mushroom Stroganoff

■ Heat the butter and olive oil in a large skillet, add the onion and garlic, and sauté gently until softened and beginning to brown.

■ Add the mushrooms to the pan and cook until softened and beginning to brown. Stir in the mustard and crème fraîche or sour cream and just heat through. Season to taste with salt and black pepper, then serve immediately, garnished with the chopped parsley.

Preparation time 10 minutes
Cooking time 10 minutes

INGREDIENTS

1   4 scallions, thinly sliced

2   1⅓ cups drained, canned corn kernels

3   1 cup sliced, drained roasted red peppers in oil (cut into thin strips)

4   4 eggs, lightly beaten

5   4 oz shredded mature cheddar cheese

PANTRY

2 tablespoons olive oil; salt and black pepper

Corn & Roasted Pepper Frittata

■ Heat the oil in a skillet with an ovenproof handle, add the scallions, corn kernels, and roasted red peppers, and cook for about 30 seconds.

■ Add the eggs, cheddar, and salt and black pepper to taste and cook over medium heat for 4–5 minutes or until the bottom is set.

■ Place the pan under a preheated hot broiler and cook for 3–4 minutes or until the omelet is golden and set. Cut into wedges and serve immediately.

SERVES 4

Preparation time 15 minutes
Cooking time 10–12 minutes

INGREDIENTS

1	12 oz dried rigatoni
2	3 zucchini, cut into ½ inch thick slices
3	2 lemon thyme sprigs
4	7 oz feta cheese, cut into cubes
5	12 green olives, pitted and coarsely chopped

PANTRY

⅓ cup olive oil; ½ lemon, for squeezing; salt and black pepper

Rigatoni with Zucchini & Feta

■ Cook the pasta in a large saucepan of salted boiling water according to the package directions until al dente. Drain thoroughly.

■ Meanwhile, put the zucchini in a large bowl and toss with 1 tablespoon of the oil. Heat a ridged grill pan over high heat until smoking. Add the zucchini slices and cook for 2–3 minutes on each side, until lightly charred and tender.

■ Return the zucchini slices to the bowl. Drizzle with the remaining oil, sprinkle with the lemon thyme sprigs, and squeeze the juice from the lemon half over the top. Season with salt and pepper.

■ Drain the pasta thoroughly and add it to the bowl with the feta and olives. Toss well to combine and serve the pasta immediately.

USE ARTICHOKES & TALEGGIO

For rigatoni with artichoke hearts and taleggio, use 2 (14 oz) cans artichoke hearts instead of the zucchini. Drain and halve the artichoke hearts, toss with 1 tablespoon oil and stir-fry with 1 tablespoon finely chopped rosemary for 2 minutes. Omit the lemon juice. Combine with the green olives and 5 oz taleggio or fontina, cut into cubes, and the cooked pasta.

Preparation time 10 minutes, plus standing
Cooking time 10–12 minutes

INGREDIENTS

1   8 very ripe small tomatoes (about 1½ lb), quartered

2   10 basil leaves

3   2 teaspoons fennel seeds

4   1 lb dried spaghetti

5   2 (5 oz) buffalo mozzarella cheese balls, cut into cubes

PANTRY

2 garlic cloves, peeled; ⅓ cup extra virgin olive oil; salt and black pepper

No-Cook-Tomato Spaghetti

■ Put the tomatoes, garlic cloves, and basil in a food processor and process until the tomatoes are finely chopped but not smooth. Transfer to a large bowl and add the fennel seeds and oil.

■ Season with salt and black pepper. Let stand for at least 15 minutes to let the flavours develop before cooking the pasta.

■ Cook the pasta in a large saucepan of salted boiling water according to the package directions until al dente. Drain, stir into the prepared tomato sauce, then toss in the mozzarella. Serve immediately.

TRY A DIFFERENT PASTA

For herbed no-cook tomato orecchiette, replace 2 of the tomatoes with sun-dried tomatoes. Coarsely shred 1 (5 oz) package of arugula and mix with the leaves from 4 sprigs of thyme. Toss with cooked orechiette and serve with mozzarella, as in the main recipe.

SERVES 6

Preparation time 40 minutes
Cooking time 50 minutes, plus standing

INGREDIENTS

1   **1 (14 oz) can diced tomatoes**

2   **6 eggplants**

3   **2 cups shredded cheddar cheese**

4   **½ cup grated Parmesan cheese**

PANTRY

¼ cup olive oil; 1 large onion, chopped;
2 garlic cloves, finely chopped; salt and
black pepper

Melanzane Parmigiana

■ To make the tomato sauce, heat half the olive oil in a skillet. Sauté the onion for about 5 minutes, then add the garlic and tomatoes and cook gently for 10 minutes. Season well with salt and black pepper and keep warm.

■ Trim the ends off the eggplants and cut them lengthwise into thick slices. Sprinkle generously with salt and set side for about 10 minutes. Wash well, drain, and pat dry on paper towels.

■ Brush the eggplant slices with the remaining oil and place them on 2 large baking sheets. Roast the eggplants in a preheated oven, at 400°F, for 10 minutes on each side, until browned and tender. Do not turn off the oven.

■ Spoon a little of the tomato sauce into an ovenproof dish, then top with a layer of roasted eggplant and some of the cheddar. Continue with the layers, finishing with the cheddar. Sprinkle the Parmesan over the top and bake for 30 minutes, until bubbling and golden brown. Remove from the oven and let stand for 5–10 minutes before serving.

SERVES 4

Preparation time 15 minutes
Cooking time 15 minutes

INGREDIENTS

1   **6 red-skinned or white round potatoes (about 1½ lb), peeled**

2   **2 teaspoons chopped rosemary**

3   **4 extra-large eggs**

4   **chopped parsley, to garnish**

PANTRY

1 onion, thinly sliced; ¼ cup olive oil;
salt and black pepper

Potato Hash Browns with Eggs

■ Using a box grater, coarsely grate the potatoes. Wrap in a clean dish towel and squeeze out the excess liquid over the sink. Transfer to a bowl and stir in the onion, rosemary, and salt and black pepper.

■ Heat half the oil in a large skillet. Divide the potato mixture into quarters and spoon into 4 (5 inch) mounds in the pan, pressing down to form patties. Cook over medium heat for 5 minutes on each side, transfer to warmed serving plates, and keep warm in a moderate oven.

■ Heat the remaining oil in the skillet for about 1 minute until hot, add the eggs, 2 at a time, and cook until the whites are bubbly and crisp looking. Serve the eggs on the hash browns, garnished with chopped parsley.

TRY POACHING THE EGGS

For hash browns with poached eggs, bring a saucepan of lightly salted water to a simmer and add 1 tablespoon white vinegar. Crack an egg into a cup. Swirl the simmering water with a large spoon, gently drop the egg into the center and cook for 2–3 minutes. Carefully remove with a slotted spoon. Repeat with the remaining eggs and finish as in the main recipe.

Preparation time 5 minutes
Cooking time 30 minutes

INGREDIENTS

1 2 (14½ oz) cans diced tomatoes

2 ¼ teaspoon dried red pepper flakes

3 2 tablespoons chopped fresh basil

4 1 lb dried spaghetti

5 ½ cup freshly grated Parmesan cheese, to serve

PANTRY

2 tablespoons extra virgin olive oil; 2 large garlic cloves, crushed; 1 teaspoon sugar; salt and black pepper

Spaghetti with Easy Tomato Sauce

■ To make the sauce, put the tomatoes, oil, garlic, sugar, and dried red pepper flakes into a saucepan. Season with salt and black pepper and bring to a boil. Lower the heat and simmer gently for 20–30 minutes, until thickened and full of flavor.

■ Stir in the basil and adjust the seasoning. Keep warm.

■ Meanwhile, cook the pasta into a saucepan of lightly salted, boiling water according to the package directions, until al dente. Drain the pasta and divide among bowls, spoon the sauce over the top, and serve with Parmesan cheese.

AN ALTERNATIVE SAUCE

For spicy tomato and olive sauce,
follow the main recipe but add
½ teaspoon dried red pepper flakes.
Stir in 1 cup pitted black ripe olives
just before the end of cooking and
heat through.

SERVES 4

Preparation time 10 minutes
Cooking time 25 minutes

INGREDIENTS

1 3 bell peppers of mixed colors, cored, seeded, and sliced into rings

2 4 tomatoes, chopped

3 1⅓ cups cubed feta cheese

4 1 teaspoon dried oregano

5 chopped flat leaf parsley, to garnish

PANTRY

¼ cup olive oil; 1 onion, thinly sliced; 4 garlic cloves, crushed; salt and black pepper

Greek Vegetable Casserole

■ Heat 3 tablespoons of the oil in a flameproof casserole dish or Dutch oven, add the onion, bell peppers, and garlic, and cook until soft and starting to brown. Add the tomatoes and cook for a few minutes, until softened. Mix in the feta and oregano, season to taste with salt and black pepper, and drizzle with the remaining oil.

■ Cover and cook in a preheated oven, at 400°F, for 15 minutes. Garnish with the parsley and serve.

Preparation time 10 minutes
Cooking time 10–15 minutes

INGREDIENTS

1   6 large ripe plum or roma tomatoes

2   1 red chile, seeded and finely diced

3   ⅔ cup finely chopped fresh basil leaves

4   12 oz dried rigatoni

5   grated Parmesan cheese, to serve (optional)

PANTRY

1 tablespoon extra-virgin olive oil; 2 garlic cloves, finely diced; ⅓ cup vegetable stock or broth; salt and black pepper

Rigatoni with Chile & Basil Tomato Sauce

■ Put the tomatoes into a bowl and pour over enough boiling water to cover. Let stand for 1–2 minutes, then drain, cut across the stem end of each tomato, and peel off the skins.

■ When cool enough to handle, cut the tomatoes in half horizontally and shake or gently spoon out the seeds, then finely dice the flesh.

■ Heat the oil in a large, nonstick skillet and add the garlic and chile. Cook over medium-low heat for 1–2 minutes or until the garlic is fragrant but not browned.

■ Add the tomatoes, vegetable stock or broth, and basil, season well and cook gently for 6–8 minutes or until thickened, stirring often.

■ Meanwhile, cook the rigatoni in a large saucepan of lightly salted boiling water according to the package directions, until al dente. Drain and toss into the tomato sauce mixture.

■ Spoon into warm bowls and serve with grated Parmesan, if desired.

HEALTHY OPTIONS

Preparation time 5 minutes
Cooking time 5 minutes

INGREDIENTS

1 ½ red chile, sliced into rings

2 1 tablespoon chopped fresh ginger root

3 1 lb bok choy, leaves separated

PANTRY

1 tablespoon peanut oil; salt; ¼ teaspoon
sesame oil

Bok Choy with Chile & Ginger

■ Heat the peanut oil in a wok over
high heat until the oil starts to shimmer.
Add the chile, ginger, and a pinch of salt
and stir-fry for 15 seconds.

■ Add the bok choy to the wok and
stir-fry for 1 minute, then add ½ cup water
and continue stirring until the bok choy is
tender and the water has evaporated. Toss
in the sesame oil and serve immediately.

SERVES 4-6

Preparation time 10 minutes, plus cooling
Cooking time 10 minutes

INGREDIENTS

1	**4 shallots, finely chopped**
2	**1 teaspoon chopped rosemary, plus extra sprigs to garnish**
3	**2 (15 oz) cans lima beans**
4	**toasted ciabatta, to serve**

PANTRY

⅓ cup extra virgin olive oil, plus extra to serve; 2 large garlic cloves, crushed; grated zest and juice of ½ lemon; salt and black pepper

Bean, Lemon & Rosemary Hummus

■ Heat the oil in a skillet, add the shallots, garlic, chopped rosemary, and lemon zest, and cook over low heat, stirring occasionally, for 10 minutes, until the shallots are softened. Let cool.

■ Transfer the shallot mixture to a blender or food processor, add the lima beans and lemon juice, and process until smooth.

■ Spread the hummus onto toasted ciabatta, garnish with rosemary sprigs, and serve drizzled with oil.

USE CHICKPEAS & CHILE

For chickpea and chile hummus, put 2 (15 oz) cans drained chickpeas in a food processor with 2 seeded and chopped red chiles, 1 large crushed garlic clove, 2 tablespoons lemon juice, and salt and black pepper to taste. Process with enough extra virgin olive oil to form a soft paste. Serve as a dip with vegetable crudités.

Preparation time 10 minutes
Cooking time 2 hours

INGREDIENTS

1   **2 (15 oz) cans cranberry beans, drained**

2   **1¼ cups tomato puree or tomato sauce**

3   **2 tablespoons molasses**

4   **2 tablespoons tomato paste**

5   **1 tablespoon Dijon mustard**

PANTRY

1 garlic clove, crushed; 1 onion, finely chopped;
2 cups vegetable stock or broth; 2 tablespoons
packed dark brown sugar; 1 tablespoon red wine
vinegar; salt and black pepper

Home Baked Beans

■ Put all the ingredients in a flameproof
casserole or Dutch oven and season with
salt and black pepper. Cover and bring
slowly to a boil.

■ Bake in a preheated oven, at 325°F,
for 1½ hours. Remove the lid and bake
for another 30 minutes, until the sauce is
syrupy. Serve with hot buttered toast, if
desired, or baked potatoes (see opposite).

JUST ADD POTATOES

The home baked beans make a great topping for baked potatoes. Scrub 4 russet potatoes, then bake them in a preheated oven, at 400°F, for about 1 hour, until cooked through. Cut lengthwise in half, season with salt and black pepper, and spoon over the beans. Grate over a little cheddar before serving. The home baked beans are even better made a day ahead and heated up before serving.

INGREDIENTS

1 1 cup bulgur wheat

2 ½ cup unsalted, shelled pistachio nuts

3 ⅓ cup chopped flat leaf parsley

4 ⅓ cup chopped mint

5 1 cup pitted prunes (dried plums), sliced

PANTRY

1 small red onion, finely chopped; 3 garlic cloves, crushed; finely grated zest and juice of 1 lemon or lime; ¼ cup olive oil; salt and black pepper

Tabbouleh with Fruit & Nuts

■ Put the bulgur wheat into a bowl, cover with plenty of boiling water, and let soak for 15 minutes.

■ Meanwhile, put the pistachio nuts in a separate bowl and cover with boiling water. Let stand for 1 minute, then drain. Rub the nuts between several thicknesses of paper towels to remove most of the skins, then peel away any remaining skins with your fingers.

■ Mix the nuts with the onion, garlic, parsley, mint, lemon or lime zest and juice, and prunes in a large bowl.

■ Drain the bulgur wheat thoroughly in a strainer, pressing out as much moisture as possible with the back of a spoon. Add to the other ingredients with the oil and toss together. Season to taste with salt and black pepper and chill until ready to serve.

A TRADITIONAL TABBOULEH

For classic tabbouleh, omit the nuts and prunes and add 6 chopped tomatoes and ½ cup chopped black ripe olives. Use only 2 garlic cloves and be sure to use a lemon not a lime.

SERVES 4

Preparation time 10 minutes
Cooking time 15–20 minutes

INGREDIENTS

1 ⅓ cup sunflower or pumpkin seeds

2 1 lb whole wheat spaghetti

3 1 small bunch of basil

4 3 cups arugula leaves

5 ⅓ cup finely grated Parmesan-style cheese, plus extra to serve (optional)

PANTRY

1 small garlic clove, coarsely chopped;
⅓ cup olive oil; 1 tablespoon lemon juice;
salt and black pepper

Basil & Arugula Pesto with Spaghetti

■ Put the seeds into a small, dry skillet and toast gently for 3–4 minutes, shaking the pan frequently, until lightly toasted and golden. Transfer to a plate to cool.

■ Cook the spaghetti in a large saucepan of lightly salted boiling water according to package directions, until al dente.

■ Meanwhile, crush the garlic together with a generous pinch of sea salt, using a mortar and pestle. Add the basil and arugula leaves, and pound until crushed to a coarse paste.

■ Add the toasted seeds and pound to a paste, then transfer to a bowl and stir in the cheese, olive oil, and lemon juice. Season to taste with plenty of black pepper and more salt, if necessary.

■ Drain the pasta and toss immediately with the pesto.

■ Divide among 4 shallow bowls and serve with extra cheese, if desired.

SERVES 4

Preparation time 10 minutes, plus standing
Cooking time 10 minutes

INGREDIENTS

1	8½ cups halved white button mushrooms (about 1¼ lb)
2	8 plum or roma tomatoes, coarsely chopped or 1 (14½ oz) can diced tomatoes
3	1 cup pitted black ripe olives
4	chopped parsley, to garnish

PANTRY

½ cup olive oil; 2 large onions, sliced;
3 garlic cloves, finely chopped; 2 tablespoons
white wine vinegar; salt and black pepper

Mushrooms à la Grecque

■ Heat 2 tablespoons of the oil in a large skillet, add the onions and garlic, and cook until soft and starting to brown. Add the mushrooms and tomatoes and cook, stirring gently, for 4–5 minutes. Remove from the heat.

■ Transfer the mushroom mixture to a serving dish and garnish with the olives.

■ Whisk the remaining oil with the vinegar in a small bowl, season to taste with salt and black pepper, and drizzle the dressin over the salad. Garnish with the chopped parsley, cover, and let stand at room temperature for 30 minutes to let the flavors mingle before serving.

INGREDIENTS

| 1 | 12 oz quick-cook pasta |

| 2 | 8 cooked beets |

| 3 | 1 cup crème fraîche or Greek yogurt |

| 4 | ¼ cup chopped chives |

| 5 | ¼ cup chopped dill |

PANTRY

salt and black pepper

Beet Pasta with Herbs

■ Cook the pasta in a large saucepan of lightly salted boiling water according to the package directions, until al dente.

■ Meanwhile, finely dice the beets and add to the pasta for the last minute of the cooking time.

■ Drain the pasta and beets and return to the saucepan. Stir in the crème fraîche or yogurt and herbs.

■ Season and serve immediately.

SERVES 4

Preparation time 10 minutes
Cooking time 35 minutes

INGREDIENTS

| 1 | 2 tablespoons mild curry paste |

| 2 | 1 (14½ oz) can diced tomatoes |

| 3 | 1 (15 oz) can chickpeas, drained |

| 4 | 4 oz curly kale |

PANTRY

3 tablespoons vegetable oil; 3 red onions, cut into wedges; 1¼ cups vegetable stock or broth; 2 teaspoons packed light brown sugar; salt and black pepper

Spiced Chickpeas with Kale

■ Heat the oil in a large saucepan and sauté the onions for 5 minutes, until beginning to brown. Stir in the curry paste and then the tomatoes, chickpeas, stock or broth, and sugar.

■ Bring to a boil, then reduce the heat, cover, and simmer gently for 20 minutes.

■ Stir in the kale and cook gently for another 10 minutes. Season to taste with salt and black pepper and serve.

SERVES 4–6

Preparation time 10 minutes, plus cooling
Cooking time 45 minutes

INGREDIENTS

1	**8 oz new potatoes, peeled and cut into ¾ inch dice**
2	**1 (7 oz) package baby spinach leaves**
3	**6 extra-large eggs**

PANTRY

2 tablespoons olive oil; 1 small onion, finely chopped; salt and black pepper

Spinach & Potato Omelet

■ Cook the potatoes in a saucepan of lightly salted boiling water until just tender; be careful not to overcook. Drain, then let cool.

■ Rinse the spinach and drain off the excess water in a colander. Put in a dry skillet over medium heat with just the water clinging to the leaves from rinsing, cover, and cook for 2–3 minutes, shaking the pan from time to time, until just wilted. Squeeze out any remaining water, then coarsely chop. Set aside.

■ Heat the oil in an 8 inch nonstick skillet with a flameproof handle (or cover the handle with aluminum foil) over low heat. Add the onion and cook, stirring occasionally, for 8–10 minutes, until softened. Add the cooled potatoes and cook, stirring, for 2–3 minutes. Add the reserved spinach and stir.

■ Beat the eggs lightly in a bowl and season with salt and black pepper. Pour into the pan over the vegetables and cook over low heat, shaking frequently, for 10–12 minutes, until set on the bottom.

■ Put the pan under a preheated medium broiler and cook for 2–3 minutes or until the top is set and lightly browned. Remove from the heat and let rest for 3–4 minutes before turning out onto a cutting board. Cut into wedges and serve immediately.

Preparation time 15 minutes
Cooking time 20-25 minutes

INGREDIENTS

1	**2 lb winter squash, such as acorn or butternut squash**
2	**½ cup walnuts, toasted**
3	**2 scallions, trimmed and chopped**
4	**2 cups arugula leaves, plus extra to serve**

PANTRY

1 large garlic clove, crushed; 3 tablespoons extra virgin olive oil, plus extra for brushing; 3 tablespoons walnut oil; salt and black pepper

Squash with Walnut Pesto

■ Cut the winter squash into 8 wedges. Remove the seeds and fiber but leave the skin on. Brush all over with olive oil, season with salt and black pepper, and spread out on a large baking sheet. Roast in a preheated oven, at 425°F, for 20-25 minutes, until tender, turning halfway through.

■ Meanwhile, make the pesto. Put the walnuts, scallions, garlic, and arugula into a food processor and process until finely chopped. With the motor running, gradually drizzle in the oils. Season the pesto with salt and black pepper.

■ Serve the roasted squash with the pesto and extra arugula leaves.

SERVES 2

Preparation time 5 minutes
Cooking time about 12 minutes

INGREDIENTS

1 8 oz dried papperdelle or other ribbon pasta

2 4 tablespoons butter

3 2 tablespoons chopped dill

4 ½ cup freshly grated Parmesan cheese

5 2 cups pea shoots or other greens, thick stems discarded

PANTRY

1 garlic clove, crushed; lemon wedges, for squeezing; salt and black pepper

Pappardelle with Pea Shoots & Dill

■ Cook the pasta in a large saucepan of lightly salted boiling water according to the package directions, until al dente. Drain and return to the pan.

■ Dot the butter onto the hot pasta and add the garlic, dill, Parmesan, and a little salt and black pepper. Stir until well mixed, then add the pea shoots or other greens and stir until slightly wilted and distributed through the pasta.

■ Serve immediately with lemon wedges for squeezing over the pasta.

SERVES 4

Preparation time 5 minutes
Cooking time 20 minutes

INGREDIENTS

1	2 leeks, cut into ½ inch pieces
2	1 orange bell pepper, seeded and cut into ½ inch chunks
3	1 red bell pepper, seeded and cut into ½ inch chunks
4	handful of flat leaf parsley, chopped

PANTRY

2 tablespoons olive oil; 3 tablespoons balsamic vinegar; salt and black pepper

Balsamic Braised Leeks & Bell Peppers

■ Heat the oil in a saucepan, add the leeks and orange and red bell peppers, and stir well.

■ Cover the pan and cook gently for about 10 minutes. Add the balsamic vinegar and cook for another 10 minutes without a lid. The vegetables should be brown from the vinegar and all the liquid should have evaporated.

■ Season well, then stir in the chopped parsley just before serving.

Preparation time 5 minutes
Cooking time 45–50 minutes

INGREDIENTS

1   **4 sweet potatoes, scrubbed**

2   **1 cup sour cream**

3   **2 scallions, trimmed and finely chopped**

4   **1 tablespoon chopped chives**

5   **4 tablespoons butter**

PANTRY

salt and black pepper

Baked Sweet Potatoes

■ Put the potatoes in a roasting pan and roast in a preheated oven, at 425°F, for 45–50 minutes, until cooked through.

■ Meanwhile, combine the sour cream, scallions, and salt and black pepper in a small bowl.

■ Cut the baked potatoes in half lengthwise, top with the butter, and spoon the sour cream mixture over them. Sprinkle with the chopped chives and serve immediately.

SWEET POTATO SKINS

For crispy sweet potato skins, let the baked sweet potatoes cool, cut into wedges, and cut out some of the soft potato, leaving a good lining inside the skin. Deep-fry in hot oil for 4–5 minutes, until crisp. Serve with sour cream and chopped chives to dip.

INGREDIENTS

1	1 lb dried spaghetti
2	2½ cups fresh or frozen shelled fava beans
3	pinch of dried red pepper flakes
4	2 tablespoons basil leaves
5	freshly grated Parmesan or pecorino cheese, to serve (optional)

PANTRY

¼ cup extra virgin olive oil; 3 garlic cloves, finely chopped; grated zest and juice of 1 lemon; salt and black pepper

Fava Bean & Lemon Spaghetti

■ Cook the pasta in a large saucepan of lightly salted boiling water according to the package directions, until al dente. Drain, reserving ¼ cup of the cooking water, and return the pasta to the pan.

■ Cook the fava beans in a separate saucepan of salted boiling water for 3–4 minutes. Drain well.

■ Meanwhile, heat the oil in a skillet, add the garlic, dried red pepper flakes, lemon zest, and salt and black pepper, and cook over low heat, stirring, for 3–4 minutes, until the garlic is soft but not browned.

■ Scrape the oil mixture into the pasta with the beans, reserved pasta cooking water, lemon juice, and basil and stir over medium heat until heated through. Serve with grated Parmesan or pecorino.

TRY IT WITH PEAS & MINT

For spaghetti with peas and mint, replace the fava beans with 2½ cups of shelled fresh peas and cook as in the recipe above, adding 2 tablespoons chopped mint instead of the basil just before serving. Frozen peas can be used instead of fresh peas.

SERVES 4

Preparation time 10 minutes
Cooking time 30 minutes

INGREDIENTS

1 ½ cup green or brown lentils

2 1 tablespoon tomato paste

3 ⅔ cup bulgur wheat

4 1 bunch of mint, chopped

5 3 tomatoes, finely chopped

PANTRY

3 cups vegetable stock or broth; juice of 1 lemon; 1 tablespoon olive oil; 2 onions, sliced; 1 teaspoon sugar; salt and black pepper

Lebanese Lentil & Bulgur Salad

■ Put the lentils, tomato paste, and stock or broth in a saucepan and bring to a boil. Reduce the heat, cover tightly, and simmer for 20 minutes. Add the bulgur wheat and lemon juice and season to taste with salt and black pepper. Cook for 10 minutes, until all the stock has been absorbed.

■ Meanwhile, heat the oil in a skillet, add the onions and sugar, and cook over low heat until deep brown and caramelized.

■ Stir the mint into the lentil and bulgur wheat mixture, then serve warm, topped with the fried onions and chopped tomato.

FOOD FOR FRIENDS

SERVES 4

Preparation time 15 minutes, plus cooling
Cooking time 40 minutes

INGREDIENTS

1	2 tablespoons unsalted butter
2	2 tablespoons chopped thyme, plus a few extra leaves to garnish
3	1 sheet of ready-to-bake puff pastry, thawed if frozen
4	2 (4 oz) goat cheese logs, each sliced into 4

PANTRY

4 large red onions, thinly sliced; 1 teaspoon packed light brown sugar; 2 teaspoons balsamic vinegar

Red Onion & Goat Cheese Tart

■ Melt the butter in a large skillet, add the onions, sugar, and chopped thyme, and cook gently for 20 minutes, stirring occasionally, until the onions start to caramelize. Stir in the vinegar and cook for 1 minute. Let cool slightly.

■ Place the pastry sheet on a nonstick baking sheet. Using a sharp knife, score a line along each side of the sheet 1 inch from the edge, being careful not to cut all the way through the pastry.

■ Spoon the caramelized onions over the pastry, within the scored border, then top with the goat cheese slices.

■ Bake in a preheated oven, at 400°F, for 20 minutes, until the pastry is risen and golden. Serve garnished with a few thyme leaves.

Preparation time 15 minutes
Cooking time 40–45 minutes, plus reheat
   20 minutes

INGREDIENTS

1	8 plum or roma tomatoes (about 1 lb)
2	1 red bell pepper, cored, seeded, and quartered
3	small bunch of sage
4	1 cup easy-cook long-grain white and wild rice mix

PANTRY

1 onion, coarsely chopped; 2 tablespoons olive oil; salt and black pepper

Sage & Tomato Pilaf

■ Cut each tomato into 8 and thickly slice the bel pepper quarters. Place in a roasting pan with the onion, then drizzle with the oil and season well. Tear some of the sage into pieces and sprinkle over the vegetables. Roast in a preheated oven, at 400°F, for 40–45 minutes, until soft.

■ Meanwhile, cook the rice in a saucepan of boiling water for 15 minutes or according to package directions, until only just cooked. Drain, rinse in cold water, and drain again. Mix the rice into the cooked tomatoes and peppers, then cover with aluminum foil. Let cool and chill until required.

■ When ready to serve, reheat in a preheated oven, at 350°F, still covered with foil for 20 minutes, until piping hot. Stir well, then spoon into bowls, sprinkle with the remaining sage leaves, and serve.

TRY A NEW FLAVOR

For squash and blue cheese pilaf, Roast 4 cups peeled, seeded, and diced butternut squash or pumpkin with 3 halved plum or roma tomatoes and onion as in the main recipe. Cook the rice for 15 minutes or according to the package directions, then drain, let cool, and chill until required. Reheat as in the main recipe, then top with 1 cup crumbled blue cheese and serve.

Preparation time 20 minutes
Cooking time 25–30 minutes

INGREDIENTS

1 6 fresh lasagna noodles

2 1 lb mixed mushrooms such as shiitake, oyster, and cremini, sliced

3 1 cup mascarpone cheese

4 4 cups baby spinach leaves

5 5 oz taleggio cheese, rind removed and cut into cubes

PANTRY

3 tablespoons olive oil; 2 garlic cloves, finely chopped; salt and black pepper

Mushroom & Spinach Lasagne

■ Place the lasagna noodles in a large roasting pan and cover with boiling water. Let stand for 5 minutes, or until tender, then drain off the water.

■ Heat the oil in a large skillet and sauté the mushrooms for 5 minutes. Add the garlic and mascarpone and turn up the heat. Cook for another 1 minute, until the sauce is thick. Season with salt and black pepper. Steam the spinach for 2 minutes or microwave until just wilted.

■ Oil an ovenproof dish about the size of 2 of the lasagna noodles placed side by side, and place 2 of the lasagna noodles over the bottom, slightly overlapping. Reserve one-third of the taleggio for the top, sprinkle a little over the pasta in the dish along with one-third of the mushroom sauce and one-third of the spinach leaves. Repeat with 2 more layers,

topping the final layer of lasagna noodles with the remaining mushroom sauce, spinach, and taleggio.

■ Bake in a preheated oven, at 400°F, for 15–20 minutes, until the cheese is golden and the lasagne piping hot.

SERVES 4

Preparation time 15 minutes
Cooking time 10 minutes

INGREDIENTS

1   **12 slices of thin baguette**

2   **2 cups marinated, pitted black ripe olives**

3   **small bunch of basil**

4   **¼ cup grated pecorino or Parmesan cheese**

PANTRY

1 garlic clove, halved; 2 tablespoons olive oil

Black Olive Tapenade Toasts

■ Toast the bread lightly on both sides, then rub one side with the garlic. Transfer to a baking sheet.

■ Finely chop the olives in a blender or food processor, then add the oil and most of the basil and blend again to make a coarse paste. Spread over the garlic toasts. Cover loosely and chill until required.

■ When ready to serve, remove the cover and cook the toasts in a preheated oven, at 375°F, for 10 minutes. Arrange on a serving plate and sprinkle with the pecorino or Parmesan and the remaining basil leaves.

SERVES 4

Preparation time 25 minutes
Cooking time 12 minutes, plus finishing

INGREDIENTS

1   **1 lb shallots, peeled**

2   **4 tablespoons butter**

3   **a few thyme sprigs**

4   **1 sheet ready-to-bake puff pastry, thawed if frozen**

PANTRY

2 tablespoons packed light brown sugar;
3 tablespoons cider vinegar; flour, for dusting;
salt and black pepper

Shallot Tart Tatin

■ Cut any large shallots in half. Melt the butter in an 8 inch skillet. Add the shallots and sauté over medium heat for 5 minutes, until just beginning to brown.

■ Add the sugar and heat for another 5 minutes or until caramelized, turning from time to time so that the shallots cook evenly. Add the vinegar, leaves from the thyme sprigs, and some seasoning and cook for 2 minutes.

■ If your skillet has a metal handle, let the shallots cool for 20 minutes in the pan; if not, transfer the onions to a heavy 8 inch buttered round cake pan.

■ Roll out the pastry on a lightly floured surface and trim to an 8 inch circle. Arrange on top of the onions and tuck down the sides of the skillet or cake pan. Cover and chill until required.

■ When ready to serve, remove the cover and bake in a preheated oven, at 400°F, for 25–30 minutes, until the pastry is well risen and golden. Let stand for 5 minutes, then loosen the edges with a knife. Cover with a serving plate or cutting board and invert the pan or cake pan onto the plate, then remove. Serve warm, cut into wedges with arugula leaves, if desired.

Preparation time 15 minutes
Cooking time 12 minutes

INGREDIENTS

1 ⅔ cup chopped flat leaf parsley

2 6 large zucchini, thickly sliced

3 8 scallions, finely sliced

4 1 lb dried linguine

5 fresh Parmesan cheese shavings, to serve

PANTRY

3 tablespoons olive oil; finely grated zest of
2 unwaxed lemons; 2 garlic cloves, crushed

Zucchini & Gremolata Linguine

■ To make the gremolata, mix 1 tablespoon
of olive oil, the lemon zest, parsley, and
garlic together in a bowl.

■ Heat the remaining oil in a nonstick
skillet over high heat, add the zucchini, and
cook, stirring frequently, for 10 minutes, or
until browned. Add the scallions and cook,
stirring, for 1–2 minutes.

■ Meanwhile, cook the pasta in a large
saucepan of lightly salted boiling water
according to the package directions,
until al dente.

■ Drain the pasta thoroughly and
transfer to a serving bowl. Add the zucchini
mixture and the gremolata and toss well.
Serve immediately with a sprinkling of
Parmesan shavings.

ASIAN FLAVORS

For green bean linguine with an Asian gremolata, use finely grated lime zest in place of the lemon zest and fresh cilantro instead of the parsley in the gremolata. Omit the zucchini and replace them with 3 cups fine green beans, cut into 1 inch lengths. Boil for 3–5 minutes. Sauté the drained beans and the scallions for 1 minute.

INGREDIENTS

1	1 lb soba noodles, cooked
2	2 carrots, finely julienned
3	6 scallions, finely shredded
4	1 red bell pepper, finely sliced
5	¼ cup dark soy sauce

PANTRY

3 tablespoons sesame oil; 3 tablespoons sesame oil; 1 tablespoon sugar; 1 teaspoon chili oil

Cold Asian Summer Soba Noodle Salad

■ Put the soba noodles into a wide bowl with the carrots, scallions, and bell pepper.

■ In a separate bowl, mix together the soy sauce, sesame oil, sugar, and chili oil, then pour the dressing over the noodle mixture.

■ Toss to mix well and serve chilled or at room temperature.

SERVES 4

Preparation time 10 minutes
Cooking time 15 minutes

INGREDIENTS

1	1½ cups mixed long grain and wild rice
2	1 cup fine green beans
3	4 oz goat cheese, sliced
4	8 baby plum or roma tomatoes, halved
5	small bunch of basil

PANTRY

¼ cupolive oil; 3 red onions, thinly sliced;
⅔ cup balsamic vinegar; salt and black pepper

Wild Rice & Goat Cheese Salad

■ Cook the rice in lightly salted boiling water according to the package directions until tender. Add the green beans for the final 2 minutes of cooking time. Drain and set aside.

■ Meanwhile, heat the oil in a large skillet and cook the onions gently for about 12 minutes or until soft and golden. Add the balsamic vinegar, season with salt and black pepper and let simmer gently for 2–3 minutes, until the mixture thickens slightly.

■ Stir the onions into the rice and beans and let cool. Once cool, sprinkle with the cheese and tomatoes and basil leaves and serve.

TRY A PEARL BARLEY SALAD

For pearl barley salad with smoked cheese, replace the rice with 2¼ cups of pearl barley and cook in boiling water for 25–35 minutes, until tender, then drain. Substitute the goat cheese for 4 oz diced smoked cheese.

SERVES 4–6

Preparation time 10 minutes
Cooking time 10–12 minutes

INGREDIENTS

1	**1–1¼ lb dried pasta twists, such as fusilli**
2	**3 ripe tomatoes**
3	**2 cups arugula leaves**
4	**¾ cup pine nuts**
5	**basil leaves, to garnish**

PANTRY

4 garlic cloves, peeled; ⅔ cup olive oil; salt and black pepper

Tomato, Pine Nut & Arugula Pesto

■ Cook the pasta in a large saucepan of salted boiling water according to the package directions until al dente.

■ Meanwhile, finely chop the tomatoes, garlic cloves, arugula, and pine nuts, then stir in the oil. Season with salt and black pepper. Transfer to a bowl.

■ Drain the pasta, add to the bowl with the pesto, and toss to combine. Serve immediately, garnished with a few basil leaves.

MAKE AN ALMOND PESTO

For tomato, parsley, and almond pesto, put 4 ripe tomatoes, 2 cloves garlic, 1 cup parsley, 1 cup almonds, and ⅔ cup olive oil into a food processor and process until smooth.

Preparation time 15 minutes
Cooking time 10 minutes

INGREDIENTS

1	2½ cups couscous

2	1 pomegranate

3	½ cup pine nuts, toasted

4	3 tablespoons chopped flat leaf parsley

5	3 tablespoons chopped fresh cilantro

PANTRY

2 tablespoons olive oil; 1 mild onion, chopped;
2 garlic cloves, crushed; 1¼ cups vegetable stock
or broth; grated zest and juice of 1 lemon;
salt and black pepper

Pilaf with Nuts, Lemon & Herbs

■ Heat the oil in a large skillet and cook
the onion and garlic for 5 minutes or until
soft. Add the stock or broth and heat, then
add the couscous. Stir, cover, and let steam
over gentle heat for 5 minutes.

■ Meanwhile, remove the seeds from the
pomegranate and set aside, working over
a bowl to catch any juice.

■ When the couscous is ready, stir in
the pine nuts and herbs and a little salt
and black pepper.

■ Mix together the pomegranate seeds
and juice and lemon zest and juice. Spoon
the dressing over the couscous just before
serving with the halloumi (see opposite),
if you desire.

QUICK & EASY HALLOUMI

For grilled marinated halloumi, slice 8 oz halloumi or Muenster into 8 pieces and marinate in the juice of 1 lemon, a dash of olive oil, and 1 fresh green chile, finely chopped. Let stand for 20 minutes before grilling in a ridged grill pan until brown and crisp. Serve 2 slices per person on top of the pilaf.

Preparation time 10 minutes
Cooking time 1 hour 10 minutes

INGREDIENTS

1	2 (14½ oz) cans diced tomatoes
2	2 tablespoon chopped basil
3	2 eggplants
4	8 oz soft goat cheese, sliced or crumbled
5	½ cup freshly grated Parmesan cheese

PANTRY

spray oil, for oiling; 2 large garlic cloves, crushed;
¼ cup extra virgin olive oil; 1 teaspoon sugar;
salt and black pepper

Eggplant & Goat Cheese Gratin

■ Lightly oil a 1¼ quart baking dish with spray oil. Put the tomatoes, garlic, half the oil, sugar, basil, and salt and black pepper into a saucepan and bring to a boil.

■ Reduce the heat and simmer for about 30 minutes, until reduced and thickened.

■ Cut each eggplant lengthwise into 6 thin slices. Season the remaining oil with salt and black pepper, then brush the eggplant slices with the seasoned oil.

■ Cook under a preheated hot broiler for 3–4 minutes on each side, until charred and tender.

■ Arrange one-third of the eggplant slices, overlapping them slightly, in the bottom of the prepared dish. Add one-third of the tomato sauce and one-third of the goat cheese and Parmesan. Repeat these layers, finishing with the 2 cheeses.

■ Bake in a preheated oven, at 400°F, for about 30 minutes until bubbling and golden bown.

SERVES 4

Preparation time 20 minutes
Cooking time 35 minutes

INGREDIENTS

1 1¼ cups Camargue red rice or long-grain brown rice

2 1 butternut squash or 1½ lb pumpkin, peeled, seeded, and diced (about 6 cups)

3 ⅓ cup finely chopped fresh basil, plus extra leaves to garnish

4 ½ cup coarsely grated Parmesan cheese, plus shavings to garnish

PANTRY

4¼ cups vegetable stock or broth; 1 tablespoon olive oil; 1 onion, finely chopped; 2 garlic cloves, finely chopped; salt and black pepper

Red Rice & Squash Risotto

■ Put the stock or broth into a large saucepan, add the rice, and simmer according to package directions.

■ Meanwhile, heat the oil in a skillet, add the onion, and cook, stirring occasionally, for 5 minutes or until softened. Add the garlic, pumpkin or squash, and a little salt and black pepper, mix together, then cover and cook over moderate heat for 10 minutes, stirring occasionally.

■ Drain the rice and reserve the cooking liquid. Stir the chopped basil into the skillet with the drained rice and grated Parmesan. Adjust the seasoning and moisten with the reserved rice liquid, if necessary.

■ Spoon into shallow dishes and serve garnished with extra basil leaves and Parmesan shavings.

SERVES 4

Preparation time 15 minutes
Cooking time 30–40 minutes

INGREDIENTS

1	3 cups finely shredded, peeled fresh ginger root
2	1 lb firm tofu (bean curd), drained, cut into ½ inch cubes
3	2 tablespoons light soy sauce
4	3 tablespoons tamarind paste or 2 tablespoons lime juice
5	small handful of cilantro leaves, to garnish

PANTRY

sunflower oil, for deep-frying; 2 garlic cloves, finely chopped; ⅓ cup coconut, palm, or brown sugar; 2 tablespoons vegetable stock or broth

Sweet & Sour Ginger Tofu

■ Heat 2 inches of oil in a wok or deep skillet over medium heat. Deep-fry all the ginger without stirring for 2–3 minutes. Move the ginger with a slotted spoon until golden brown, then drain on paper towels.

■ Lower the tofu cubes into the oil, in batches, and deep-fry for 5–6 minutes, until lightly browned and soft inside. Drain on paper towels.

■ Remove most of the oil, leaving 1½ tablespoons in the wok. Stir-fry the garlic over medium heat for 1–2 minutes or until lightly browned. Add the sugar, soy sauce; stock, broth, or water; and tamarind paste or lime juice. Stir over low heat until slightly thickened. Taste and adjust the seasoning, if necessary. Add the tofu and most of the crispy ginger and mix together.

■ Spoon into 4 warm serving bowls and garnish with the remainder of the crispy ginger.

DESSERTS

SERVES 4

Preparation time 10 minutes
Cooking time 12–15 minutes

INGREDIENTS

1 4 egg yolks

2 ⅔ cup cream sherry

3 large pinch of ground cinnamon

4 1 (15 oz) can black cherries in syrup

5 2 amaretti cookies, crumbled, to decorate

PANTRY

⅔ cup superfine or granulated sugar

Cherry & Cinnamon Zabaglione

■ Pour 2 inches of water into a medium saucepan and bring to a boil. Cover with a large heatproof bowl, making sure that the water does not touch the bottom of the bowl. Reduce the heat so that the water is simmering, then add the egg yolks, sugar, sherry, and cinnamon to the bowl. Whisk for 5–8 minutes, until thick and foamy and the custard leaves a trail when the whisk or beaters are lifted above the mixture.

■ Drain off some of the cherry syrup and then transfer the cherries and just a little of the syrup to a small saucepan. Warm through, then spoon into 4 dessert glasses.

■ Pour the warm zabaglione over the top and decorate with the amaretti cookies. Serve immediately.

SERVES 4

Preparation time 10 minutes
Cooking time 7–8 minutes

INGREDIENTS

1	3 tablespoons unsalted butter
2	3 sweet, crisp apples, cored and thickly sliced
3	2 large pinches ground cinnamon
4	4 prepared crepes, 8 inches in diameter (follow directions on a pancake mix package) or 4 waffles
5	¼ cup chocolate and hazelnut spread

PANTRY

confectioners' sugar, for dusting

Chocolate Apple Crepes

■ Melt half the butter in a large skillet, then add the apple slices and sauté for 3-4 minutes, stirring and turning until hot and lightly browned. Sprinkle with the cinnamon.

■ Separate the pancakes, then spread them with the chocolate spread. Divide the apples among the pancakes, spooning them to cover half of each pancake. Fold the uncovered sides over the apples.

■ Heat the remaining butter in the skillet, add the pancakes, and saute for a couple of minutes on each side to warm the pancakes through. Transfer to shallow plates and dust with confectioners' sugar.

■ Alternatively, heat the waffles according to the package directions, spread each with the chocolate spread, top with the apple mixture, dividing it evenly among the waffles, and dust with confectioners' sugar before serving.

TRY IT WITH PEACHES

For peach melba crepes or waffles, cook 2 large, thickly sliced peaches in the butter instead of the apples, omitting the cinnamon. Spread the pancakes or waffles with ¼ cup raspberry preserves, then add the peaches and fold, if using crepes. Warm through, then serve sprinkled with fresh raspberries, a dusting of confectioners' sugar, and a scoop of ice cream.

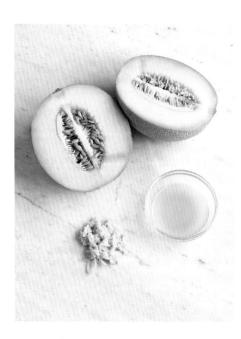

SERVES 4

Preparation time 15 minutes, plus freezing

INGREDIENTS

1	1 large ripe honeydew melon or canteloupe, chilled
2	1 tablespoon peeled and finely grated fresh ginger root
3	juice of 2 limes

PANTRY

¾ cup superfine or granulated sugar

Melon, Ginger & Lime Sorbet

■ Cut the melon in half and remove and discard the seeds, then coarsely chop the flesh; you need about 3 cups. Put into a blender or food processor with the sugar, ginger, and lime juice, then blend until smooth.

■ Transfer the sorbet to an ice cream maker and process according to the manufacturer's instructions. If you don't have an ice cream maker, place the mixture in a freezer-proof container and freeze for 2–3 hours or until ice crystals appear on the surface. Beat with a handheld electric mixer until smooth, then return to the freezer. Repeat this process two times until you have a fine-textured sorbet and freeze until firm.

■ Remove the sorbet from the freezer about 10 minutes before serving. Serve, scooped into glasses with a thin cookie.

SERVES 2

Preparation time 5 minutes, plus freezing

INGREDIENTS

1 2 cups frozen mixed summer berries, such as raspberries, blackberries, blueberries and/or halved or quartered hulled strawberries

2 ⅓ cup blackberry syrup

3 2 tablespoons Kirsch

4 1 tablespoon lime juice

Summer Berry Sorbet

■ Put a shallow plastic container in the freezer to chill. Process the frozen berries, syrup, Kirsch, and lime juice in a food processor or blender to a smooth puree. Be careful not to over-process, because this will soften the mixture too much.

■ Spoon into the chilled container and freeze for at least 25 minutes. Spoon into serving bowls and serve.

SWITCH TO RASPBERRIES

For raspberry sorbet: replace
the main recipe ingredients with
2 cups frozen raspberries, ⅓ cup
elderflower syrup or cordial
(available online), 2 tablespoons of
crème de cassis, and 1 tablespoon
of lemon juice. Proceed as in the
main recipe.

Preparation time 20 minutes, plus cooling
  and chilling
Cooking time 35 minutes

INGREDIENTS

1	10 oz good-quality bitterdark chocolate with chile, broken into pieces
2	1¼ sticks unsalted butter, diced
3	6 eggs, separated
4	1 red chile, thinly sliced
5	grated zest and juice of 1 lime

PANTRY

1 cup plus 2 tablespoons superfine or
granulated sugar

Chocolate & Chile Mousse Cake

■ Line the bottom of an 8 inch springform cake pan with nonstick parchment paper. Melt the chocolate and butter in a heatproof bowl set over a saucepan of gently simmering water, stirring occasionally, making sure the water doesn't touch the bottom of the bowl.

■ Meanwhile, whisk the egg yolks with ⅔ cup of the sugar in a bowl with a handheld electric mixer until pale and thick. Stir in the melted chocolate mix.

■ Whisk the egg whites in a separate large, grease-free bowl until they form soft peaks. Fold a couple of tablespoons of the egg white into the chocolate mixture to loosen, then fold in the remaining egg white with a metal spoon.

■ Pour the batter into the prepared pan and bake in a preheated oven, at 350°F, for 20 minutes. Remove from the oven, cover with aluminum foil (to prevent a crust forming), and let cool. Chill in the refrigerator for at least 4 hours or overnight.

■ Make the syrup. Combine the chile, lime zest and juice, and remaining sugar with ⅔ cup water in a small saucepan and heat over low heat, stirring, until the sugar has dissolved.

■ Bring to a boil, then simmer for about 10 minutes, until syrupy. Let cool. Remove the cake from the refrigerator 30 minutes before serving in slices, with the syrup poured over the top.

SERVES 4

Preparation time 15 minutes
Cooking time about 10 minutes

INGREDIENTS

1 2 eggs

2 ⅔ cup milk

3 4 crisp, sweet apples, cored and thickly sliced

4 1 cup frozen blackberries

PANTRY

1 cup all-purpose flour; ¼ cup superfine or granulated sugar; sunflower oil, for deep-frying; confectioners' sugar, for dusting

Apple Fritters with Blackberry Sauce

■ Separate one egg and put the white into one bowl and the yolk and the whole egg into a second bowl. Add the flour and half the sugar to the second bowl. Whisk the egg white until if forms soft peaks, then use the same whisk or mixer to beat the flour mixture until smooth, gradually beating in the milk. Fold in the egg white.

■ Pour the oil into a deep, heavy saucepan until it comes one-third of the way up the side, then heat until it reaches 350–375ºF, or until a cube of bread browns in 30 seconds. Dip a few apple slices in the batter and turn gently to coat. Lift out one slice at a time and lower carefully into the oil. Deep-fry, in batches, for 2–3 minutes, turning until evenly golden. Remove with a slotted spoon and drain on paper towels.

■ Meanwhile, put the blackberries and the remaining sugar into a small saucepan with 2 tablespoons water and heat for 2–3 minutes, until hot. Arrange the fritters on serving plates, spoon the blackberry sauce around, and dust with a little confectioners' sugar.

MAKE BANANA FRITTERS

For banana fritters with raspberry
sauce, use 4 thickly sliced bananas
in place of the apples. Use 1 cup
of frozen raspberries instead of
the blackberries. Proceed as in the
main recipe.

SERVES 4

Preparation time 10 minutes
Cooking time 10–12 minutes

INGREDIENTS

1   8 firm but ripe fresh figs

2   3 oz soft goat cheese

3   8 mint leaves

4   5 cups baby arugula leaves

PANTRY

3 tablespoons extra virgin olive oil; 1 teaspoon lemon juice; salt and black pepper

Baked Figs with Goat Cheese

■ Cut a cross in the top of each fig without cutting through the bottom. Put 1 teaspoonful of the goat cheese and a mint leaf in each fig. Transfer to a roasting pan, then season with salt and black pepper and drizzle with 2 tablespoons of the oil.

■ Bake in a preheated oven, at 375°F, for 10–12 minutes, until the figs are soft and the cheese has melted.

■ Put the baby arugula leaves in a bowl. Whisk together the remaining oil, lemon juice, salt, and black pepper and drizzle the dressing over the greens. Serve with the figs.

SERVES 4

Preparation time 10 minutes

INGREDIENTS

1	1 lb fresh strawberries
2	4–5 lavender flower stems, plus extra to decorate
3	1⅔ cups Greek yogurt
4	4 store-bought meringue shells

PANTRY

2 tablespoons confectioners' sugar, plus extra for dusting

Strawberry & Lavender Crush

■ Reserve 4 small strawberries for decoration. Hull the remainder, put in a bowl with the confectioners sugar, and mash together with a fork. Alternatively, process the strawberries and confectioners' sugar in a food processor or blender to a smooth puree. Pull off the lavender flowers from the stems and crumble them into the puree to taste.

■ Put the yogurt in a bowl, crumble in the meringues, then lightly mix together. Add the strawberry puree and fold together with a spoon until marbled. Spoon into 4 dessert glasses.

■ Cut the reserved strawberries in half, then use together with the lavender flowers to decorate the desserts. Lightly dust with confectioners' sugar and serve immediately.

SERVES 4

Preparation time 5 minutes, plus chilling
Cooking time 3–4 minutes

INGREDIENTS

1	6 oz semisweet chocolate, broken into pieces
2	½ cup heavy cream
3	3 eggs, separated
4	unsweetened cocoa powder, for dusting

Rich Chocolate Mousse

■ Put the chocolate and cream into a heatproof bowl set over a saucepan of gently simmering water, making sure the water does not touch the bottom of the bowl, and stir until the chocolate has melted. Remove the bowl from the heat and let the mixture cool for 5 minutes, then beat in the egg yolks one at a time.

■ Whisk the egg whites in a separate, clean bowl until stiff, then lightly fold into the chocolate mixture until combined. Spoon the mousse into 4 dessert glasses or cups and chill for 2 hours. Dust with cocoa powder before serving.

ADD A CLASSIC TWIST

For chocolate and orange mousse, follow the main recipe, but add the grated zest of 1 large orange and 2 tablespoons Grand Marnier to the melted chocolate and cream. Proceed as in the main recipe.

SERVES 4

Preparation time 15 minutes, plus chilling
Cooking time 30 minutes

INGREDIENTS

1 2 eggs, plus 2 extra egg yolks

2 1⅔ cups coconut milk

3 ½ cup low-fat milk

4 1 cup raspberries

5 1 teaspoon butter, for greasing

PANTRY

⅔ cup granulated sugar; 2 tablespoons superfine
or granulated sugar

Coconut Crème Caramel

■ Heat the granulated sugar with
½ cup water in a small saucepan, stirring
occasionally, until the sugar has just
dissolved. Bring to a boil and cook, without
stirring, for 5 minutes, until golden.

■ Take the pan off the heat, add
2 tablespoons of boiling water, then stand
well back, tilting the pan to mix, until the
bubbles have subsided. Divide the caramel
between four 1-cup metal dessert molds,
then swirl the caramel over the inside.
Put the molds into a roasting pan.

■ Whisk the eggs, egg yolks, and
2 tablespoons of sugar together to mix.
Pour the coconut milk and milk into a
saucepan and bring just to a boil,
then gradually whisk into the eggs.
Strain into the molds.

■ Pour ½ cup hot (not boiling) water into
the roasting pan to come halfway up the
sides of the molds. Cover the tops loosely
with buttered aluminum foil, then bake in a
preheated oven, at 325°F, for 30 minutes,
until just set. Remove from the oven and let
the molds stand in the water for 10 minutes.
Lift them out, let cool, then chill for 4 hours
or longer until required.

■ When ready to serve, dip the bottom
of the molds into boiling water for about
10 seconds, loosen, then turn out onto
rimmed serving plates. Decorate
with raspberries.

MAKE IT CHOCOLATY

For chocolate custard desserts, whisk 2 eggs, 2 egg yolks, and ¼ cup superfine or granulated sugar together. Heat ⅔ cup heavy cream and 2 cups milk in a saucepan with 5 oz semisweet chocolate, stirring until melted. Whisk into the eggs, then pour into small heatproof dishes. Cook as in the main recipe for 20–25 minutes. Cool and serve with cream.

Preparation time 5 minutes
Cooking time 8–10 minutes

INGREDIENTS

1	4 bananas, unpeeled
2	½ cup fat-free Greek yogurt
3	¼ cup oatmeal rolled oats
4	1 cup blueberries
5	honey, to serve

Grilled Bananas with Blueberries

■ Heat a ridged grill pan over medium-hot heat, add the unpeeled bananas, and grill for 8–10 minutes, or until the skins are beginning to blacken, turning occasionally.

■ Transfer the bananas to serving dishes and, using a sharp knife, cut open lengthwise.

■ Spoon the yogurt over the bananas and sprinkle with the oats and blueberries. Serve immediately, drizzled with a little honey.

MAKE A YOGURT

For oat, ginger, and golden raisin yogurt, mix ½ teaspoon ground ginger with ½ cup of yogurt in a bowl. Sprinkle with 2–4 tablespoons packed light brown sugar, according to taste, the oatsl and ¼ cup golden raisins. Let stand for 5 minutes before serving.

SERVES 8

Preparation time 35 minutes, plus cooling
Cooking time 25 minutes

INGREDIENTS

1	**4 egg whites**
2	**1 teaspoon cornstarch**
3	**1⅓ cups dried apricots**
4	**⅔ cup heavy cream**
5	**⅔ cup fromage blanc or Greek yogurt**

PANTRY

1¼ cups superfine or granulated sugar, plus extra for sprinkling; 1 teaspoon white wine vinegar

Apricot Meringue Swirl

■ Whisk the egg whites until stiff peaks form. Gradually whisk in the sugar, then whisk for another few minutes until the mixture is thick and glossy.

■ Mix the cornstarch and vinegar together until they are smooth. Fold into the meringue mixture.

■ Spoon into a 13 × 9 inch jellyroll pan lined with nonstick parchment paper snipped diagonally into the corners and standing a little above the top of the sides. Spread level. Bake in a preheated oven, at 375°F, for 10 minutes, until lightly brown and well risen. Reduce the heat to 325°F, for 5 minutes, until just firm to the touch and the top is slightly cracked.

■ Cover a clean dish towel with nonstick parchment paper and sprinkle with a little sugar. Turn the hot meringue out onto the paper, remove the pan, and let cool for 1–2 hours. Meanwhile, simmer the apricots in 1¼ cups water for 10 minutes, until tender. Cool, then puree until smooth.

■ Peel the lining paper off the meringue when ready to serve, then spread with the apricot puree. Whip the cream until it forms soft swirls, then fold in the fromage blanc or yogurt and spoon it over the apricot puree.

■ Roll up the meringue to make a log shape, starting from a short side and using the paper to help. Transfer to a serving plate and cut into thick slices to serve.

TRY DIFFERENT FRUIT

For kiwi and passion fruit swirl,
make the meringue as in the main
recipe. Fill with 1¼ cups whipped
heavy cream, then sprinkle with
3 chopped kiwi fruits and the seeds
from 3 passion fruits.

Preparation time 15 minutes, plus cooling
and chilling

INGREDIENTS

1   **5 oz good-quality milk chocolate, broken into pieces**

2   **¾ cup dulce de leche (caramel sauce)**

3   **1 cup heavy cream**

4   **1½ oz bar milk chocolate with golden sponge candy (honeycomb toffee), coarsely chopped, plus extra to decorate**

Caramel & Sponge Candy Mousse

■ Melt the milk chocolate in a heatproof bowl set over a saucepan of gently simmering water, stirring occasionally, making sure that the water doesn't touch the bottom of the bowl. Let cool slightly.

■ Put the dulce de leche (caramel sauce) into a bowl with the cream and whisk with a handheld electric mixer until the mixture starts to thicken and leaves a trail.

■ Stir a little of the caramel mixture into the melted chocolate, then fold the chocolate mixture into the caramel mixture until well combined. Stir in the chocolate sponge candy.

■ Spoon into 6 small glasses and chill for 15–30 minutes (no longer, otherwise the honeycomb will start to dissolve). Decorate with a little extra chocolate sponge candy before serving.

SERVES 6

Preparation time 20 minutes, plus cooling
  and freezing
Cooking time 4 minutes

INGREDIENTS

 **½ cup fresh mint, plus a few sprigs
to decorate**

PANTRY

1 cup superfine or granulated sugar; pared zest
and juice of 3 lemons; confectioners' sugar, to dust

Mint Granita

■ Put the superfine or granulated sugar
and 1¼ cups of water into a saucepan, add
the lemon zest, and gently heat until the
sugar has dissolved. Increase the heat and
boil for 2 minutes.

■ Tear the tips off the mint stems and
finely chop to give about 3 tablespoons,
then reserve. Add the larger mint leaves
and stems to the hot syrup and let stand
for 1 hour to cool and for the flavors
to develop.

■ Strain the syrup into a small bowl, add
the chopped mint, and top up to 2½ cups
with extra cold water. Pour into a small
roasting pan and freeze the mixture for
2–3 hours or until mushy.

■ Break up the ice crystals with a fork,
then return to the freezer for another
2–3 hours, breaking up with a fork once or
twice until the mixture is the consistency
of crushed ice. Serve now, spooned into
small glass glasses, decorated with tiny
sprigs of mint dusted with confectioners'
sugar, or leave in the freezer until required.

■ If leaving in the freezer, let soften
for 15 minutes before serving. If frozen
overnight or longer, break up with a
fork before serving.

INDEX

PICTURE CREDITS

Octopus Publishing Group 7, 29, 33, 165, 185, 189; Frank Adam 59; Stephen Conroy 9, 47, 69, 81, 83, 85, 91, 97, 113, 119, 131, 149; Will Heap 8, 37, 99, 103, 115, 139, 147; William Lingwood 27, 53, 75, 121, 145, 157, 163, 173, 177; David Loftus 125; Lis Parsons 39, 45, 49, 60–61, 65, 73, 77, 87, 89, 132-133, 153; William Reavell 35, 109, 111; William Shaw 20-21, 25, 51, 55, 57, 71, 79, 117, 123, 135, 137, 141, 142, 160–161, 167, 171, 181, 183, 187; Eleanor Skan 159; Simon Smith 23, 43; Ian Wallace 5, 6, 31, 41, 63, 67, 93, 95, 100-101, 105, 107, 127, 129, 151, 155, 169, 175, 179.